✓ Y0-DBY-617

Twilight Chase

Emma Raven

Twilight Chase

ony

Copyright: © 2011 by Emma Raven
Cover and inside illustrations: © Jennifer Bell
Cover layout: Stabenfeldt AS

Typeset by Roberta L. Melzl
Editor: Bobbie Chase
Printed in Germany, 2011

ISBN: 978-1-934983-81-2

Stabenfeldt Inc.
225 Park Avenue South
New York, NY 10003
www.pony.us

Available exclusively through PONY

Chapter 1

"There. Look! White cliffs!"

Liv flung her arm out across the sea to the horizon.
"Can you see?"

I peered into the distance and saw the line of chalk cliffs
that seemed to have appeared from nowhere. They really
were white. The sky was a clear blue and the sun shone on
our backs as we hung over the railings of the ferry, which
was plowing through the channel. I stared down at the froth
being cast aside on the surface of the sea, finding it oddly
hypnotic. Soon we would arrive in another new place, with
all of the horses. I was on my way to shoot my second
movie and, if it was possible, I was even more excited than I
had been the last time. I just couldn't wait.

I smiled to myself and blinked my gaze away from the
waves below.

"How long until we dock?"

Ryan was beside me. He checked his watch.

"About twenty minutes."

I smiled across at the girls, Liv and Rachel, my best friends. Rachel hunched up her shoulders and shot me an excited grin, her pretty, brown eyes dancing with anticipation.

"Come on," she said. "We should go back down to the trailer."

The girls headed off along the deck as I turned to Ryan. He was still gazing out at the distant coastline and I stole a moment to stare at his profile. He had the fine Latin features of a model from an expensive perfume ad. His gently waving black hair fell forward onto his forehead, and he had lovely olive skin. Unfortunately Ryan's not my boyfriend. I don't think he thinks about anything except horses from the moment he wakes up in the morning.

I stopped staring just as he turned around to me, his features betraying the end of a little frown. It was Ryan's natural, slightly brooding look.

"Come on," I said brightly. "This is going to be great."

He smiled at me. "I bet we find Dad before those two. They have no idea where they're going."

I laughed and headed for the heavy doors across the deck behind us. We descended five levels of stairs in a leisurely fashion. Just as we reached the last flight we heard the sound of two sets of feet scrambling hurriedly down the stairs toward us. Ryan and I looked at each other as Liv and Rachel eventually came flying into view.

"You could have told us the right way!" Liv said, her light blue eyes wide.

"You'd still have gotten lost," Ryan joked dryly.

Liv glared and put her hands on her hips and flicked her curly blonde hair out of her face.

"No we wouldn't!"

"You got lost in the gas station this morning! Come on. I can hear the engines moving us into the berth." Ryan laughed as he stepped onto the car deck.

Liv tutted and followed.

"He'd better not be like this the whole trip," she huffed.

It wouldn't be the same if Ryan and Liv didn't argue, nonstop. They just seemed to wind each other up. I think it was because they used to date each other. Their bickering was funny – most of the time.

I heard the rumbling sound of the ferry's engines changing as the huge ship moved toward the dock. The car deck smelled badly of exhaust fumes and I would be really glad when we were out in the fresh air again.

Mr. Vazquez, Ryan's dad, was back in the driver's seat, finishing a cup of coffee. I joined Rachel, who is Ryan's sister, in the back with our horses, smiling instantly as I always did when I laid eyes on them. Five pairs of eyes greeted me. Toby the huge, gray leader of the pack, Chokky and Velvet, Rachel's bright bays, Red, Ryan's wonderful chestnut and Luce, their black stallion whom I looked after and rode – or, as I like to think of him, my horse.

"We're all happy back here," Rachel said. "But he wants a hug." She nodded at Luce.

I reached over and placed my arm around his neck and he snorted gently into my ear, fanning my hair against my cheek.

"Are you going to be good?" I asked him. Luce shook his head and I heard Rachel giggle. "Great," I said.

I patted his silky neck and stroked his nose so he could see me with his gentle stare, out of those huge almond shaped eyes – the same ones that I hadn't been able to tear myself away from the very first time I saw him in the field.

All of our horses were stallions. They make perfect stunt horses. Luce is a raven-black Lusitano. He's different from the others, a little naughty and strange and I love him more than I can ever tell you. He was out of control when he first joined Mr. Vazquez's stables, after Ryan bought him on a whim, thinking he looked the part. Naughty behavior isn't allowed in this kind of work, but he had a good reason to be acting up. He'd been treated really badly. He liked me right away, though. It was the perfect partnership. He behaved when I rode him and got a second chance in his new home to train to be a stunt horse. I got to ride an amazing horse and become part of the team, and I got to hang out with the cute Ryan!

Luce is still naughty when Mr. Vazquez isn't looking, but he does it as more of a joke these days. If someone is kicking the door, it's probably him. I like to call it spirit, but I don't encourage him. He has a look that you will never forget when he fixes you with his gentle eyes. He looks like something out of a fairy tale.

I felt a sudden little jumble of nerves in my stomach as I thought about what I would be doing in the coming days. A little worry about my vaulting had slowly been creeping in. I'd only been doing it for six months, and hoped that Luce would be okay once those cameras started rolling.

Suddenly another horsey face was right before my eyes as Red pushed his way into the scene. I fussed over the two friends while Rachel did the same with the others.

"All fine, nothing to report," she concluded brightly. "I think they actually *like* being in the trailer."

"It's because they know we're going somewhere cool," I said.

"They'll love the place we're going to. It's in a valley, with woods. I don't think the sea is very far, either."

I kissed the two horse faces vying for my attention and we made our way back to the cab. I sank down into the back seat just as the ferry's ramp was being lowered, flooding the deck with sunshine. Mr. Vazquez and everyone else turned on their ignitions, and we rolled forward.

"Remember to drive carefully. They said the roads are winding," Liv said to Mr. Vazquez.

"I try," came the usual dry response, in a heavy Spanish accent. "Who is my map reader?" Mr. Vazquez refused to get a GPS, insisting they were "for idiots."

"I am," Liv called, grabbing the map from Ryan's hands.

"Hey!" he shouted.

Mr. Vazquez shot them a look.

"Anyone map reading. Except you," he said to Liv.

Ryan wordlessly took the map from Liv as she folded her arms and went into a sulk.

"We'll end up in the wrong country if you're in charge," Ryan told her.

Mr. Vazquez chuckled. "You can do it when you know left from right," he said to Liv, whose sulk lasted until she saw a cute boy hanging around by the docks two minutes later.

It was the nicest, hottest, sunny August day with not a cloud in the sky. The first beach I spied was full of people, many of them in the sea. The sight just made me feel really happy, thinking of all the families on vacation together. I would have loved to be with my mom and dad – and Tony who lived with us and worked with my dad. He was my best friend and Rachel's boyfriend.

This was the second time I'd been asked to come on a movie shoot with the horses and everyone from the stables. They were my family too now. I couldn't imagine life without them. I'd learned so much and found I loved something more than I ever thought possible. I was great with horses. I often wondered how many people could be but never got to find out for themselves, because they never went near a stable. I felt sorry for people who never got to be around horses.

Having Ryan around was an extra bonus. I got to hang out with him all day, and the girls were tons of fun. We were all BFFs. Mr. Vazquez kept us all in check. He was really strict. Apparently he came from a long line of strict people. Ryan told me that. Fair enough, I thought, especially since we look after highly trained stunt horses. There was no fooling around when you were at his stables and with his horses. Mr. Vazquez suffers no fools. Our silly arguments were just funny most of the time, though, and we didn't often get into trouble. Being on a movie set was fabulous, nerve-wracking and amazing. I was so lucky.

I settled down to watch the scenery pass by. It was like home, really, except for the buildings and the road signs. I liked the way the fields were separated by knotted rows of old hedges. Occasionally we spotted the sea to our right and then, after a couple of hours, we turned off the highway and the landscape quickly became open fields, with nothing else in sight. Ryan peered more closely at the map. We had to make sure we didn't get stuck on any tight bends. That was one of the reasons Liv wasn't allowed to map read. She had gotten us lost three times with wrong directions. The third time it happened Mr. Vazquez didn't speak to her for days. We passed through a pretty village and then the roads became narrower, with just the occasional house or farm dotted around.

"It's just down here, I think," Ryan said eventually and pointed ahead to where the single-lane road descended into the woods. Mr. Vazquez slowed right down as the leafy canopy blocked out the sun. After a short distance the trailer rumbled over an ancient stone bridge, where the road leveled out and the trees receded behind us.

We had arrived at what looked like a tiny farm at the bottom of a valley. All the buildings were made of crumbling yellow stone and were strung out along a trail that ran alongside the river. The road across the bridge was just a wide, earth-baked track. Mr. Vazquez turned left onto it easily and then right into the stable yard through a large gap. There was no sign of anyone as the engine cut out and silence took over.

We all got out and sniffed the air. Mr. Vazquez headed straight for the horse boxes on two sides of the yard to look around. He peered over a half door and nodded to himself.

"There is a little for us to do," he said. I didn't mind. I was ready for some activity after the journey. Liv and Rachel investigated the shed.

"It's all here," Rachel said.

"Anyone seen the faucet?" Ryan called from over by the open-sided barn. I followed him up the wooden steps to the bales of sweet smelling hay.

"Faucet's here," Liv called as Mr. Vazquez emerged with an armful of rakes from the shed, struggling slightly, but I knew better than to let even the faintest grin cross my face. Like a hawk he turned his head up to Ryan and me, idly admiring the view from up in the loft. We both moved toward the stairs to help out.

"This is weird," Rachel said, as we gathered at the rear

of the trailer. "It's like someone built a film set of a farm. Doesn't anyone live here?"

Ryan shrugged.

"An old man lived here for years on his own. He died and someone rich bought the whole thing. They're making it into a vacation place. Look," he pointed to the three-storey farmhouse that overlooked the stables. "All those windows are new. The bulldozers are coming after we leave, to put a pool in, and I bet the stables will go too."

I made a face. "Like a kind of exclusive vacation home."

Ryan began pushing the trailer's bolts back.

"Yup. The first thing the new owners did was hire this place out to the film company who hired us."

"But no one else is staying here, are they?"

"No. They're all in a hotel in that last town we passed." Ryan told me.

He lowered the ramp and stood back as Mr. Vazquez took charge of the unloading.

"When did the old guy die?"

"Last year, I think. The place was a wreck."

I nodded, wondering how he knew all this stuff.

I began thinking about the poor old man living here all alone. I hope he hadn't always been alone. It felt like a sad, odd little place with some other little houses. Like an abandoned village. I looked over into the empty horse boxes, the doors now open and ready for their new guests. The shavings were fresh. They just needed banking.

I gazed over the roof of the boxes at the field that rose steeply behind them. There seemed to be a trail up the side, and I was looking forward to exploring all the open space. Then I saw the silhouette of a man in the shadow of the first line of trees. He was looking down upon us from the top of the hill.

"You did say the old man had died, didn't you?" I asked Ryan, frowning.

"Yes. Why? Seen a ghost already, Salma?"

Ryan was looking at me strangely, despite his sarcastic tone.

I glanced back up the hill but the figure was no longer there.

"Did you see him too, up there under the trees near the ridge?"

Ryan nodded. "He's probably wondering what all the activity is all of a sudden."

I glanced back up the hill, trying to peer into the trees. Like the woods surrounding my house back home, the first line of tall sycamores was a dense barrier. I knew I would be seeing the stranger again sooner or later, but before I had time to think about it any more I heard my horse stepping into the yard with a theatrical whinny.

I moved quickly to help Ryan grab hold of Luce's head collar as he reared, his ears back and his eyes darting. He calmed instantly as I started talking to him, but as he looked at us, I could see there was a huge contrast to the calm and happy horse I had seen in the trailer on the ferry.

I felt a familiar bolt of nerves shoot through me; fear of what was to come if Luce decided he didn't like this place. I hated it when he was anxious. He'd spent enough of his life like that before we got him. I saw Mr. Vazquez's stern expression, casting his judgmental eye over my black stallion as he began to shake his head. Luce was nearly always on probation.

I whispered in his ear (Luce's, not Mr. Vazquez's!) and rubbed the front of his face tenderly before leading him over toward the boxes and tying him to the hoop. He seemed to have recovered some composure, but his ears were still back and he continued to shake his head.

"There's something he doesn't like about this place," Ryan said.

I turned around toward Mr. Vazquez. "He's fine," I called, laughing weakly, "just announcing his arrival."

Mr. Vazquez nodded and disappeared into a box with a rake.

I groomed Luce with his best brush and felt the tension in his muscles subside a little. I rubbed the front of his face and was happy to see his eyelids drop. The others were fine, all being looked after and drinking water. So what was it with my horse?

Mr. Vazquez and Rachel banked up the shavings efficiently, and soon all the horses were checking out their new homes. I stayed with Luce, my mind whirring as I wondered what vibes he had picked up on in this odd little place. I knew better than to ignore his sixth sense.

❄   ❄   ❄   ❄

"It's lovely," Liv said. She was talking about the farmhouse. We were in the hall. I must have walked with them around to the front door by the river and up the little steps without even realizing. There was a faint smell of fresh paint as we glanced around the welcoming space.

Liv and Rachel had already raced upstairs.

"The rooms are great," Rachel called as Ryan and I headed for the stairs.

"This is yours," Liv said to Ryan, ushering him through a door to the right at the top of the stairs.

"Who made you housekeeper?" he asked.

"Oh? Do you want to be in the girls' room?" Liv replied cheekily.

Ryan rolled his eyes and shut the door of his room in our faces.

"Our room is *huge*," Rachel said as she linked her arm through mine and led me across the landing. She wasn't kidding.

"We'll need a microphone to talk to each other," I laughed.

The decoration was modern and simple and there were three beds around the edge of the room with a large space in the middle. It felt like an aunt's cozy guest room. I was relieved. From the vibe down in the yard, I had expected creaking wooden floorboards and unusual drafts.

"I'm glad we're all together," Rachel said, checking her reflection in the mirror and smoothing down her already sleek high ponytail. "It'll be fun."

I stood behind her and tried to rake my fingers a little through the clumps of my hair. My eyes looked bright despite the tiring journey and it looked like I had a slight glow from catching the sun on the ferry.

"It'll be fun," I added. "Even with this crazy person," I winked at Liv. There had been a time when we didn't get along, but these days she mostly made me laugh. We were pals now.

"Ryan thinks I'm an idiot," she said huffily.

"You are," I told her, watching her haughty expression settle on me. "But you're a funny idiot." I gave her petite frame a hug and suddenly realized how dark it had gotten outside.

Rachel was fiddling with a fancy brass floor lamp, trying to find the switch. We laughed at her efforts and then broke into hissing giggles as she accidentally stepped on the floor switch and turned it on.

And then the scream of a terrified horse rang out into the night, instantly wiping the grins off our faces.

Chapter 2

We froze there for a moment, staring at each other across the room, waiting to see if the scream came again. I expected to hear Ryan leave his room immediately to head down to the yard but instead, when we all dashed out onto the landing, he was coming up the stairs, out of breath.

"Who was it, Ry?" we all asked at once, appearing wide-eyed in a line in front of him.

Ryan seemed bewildered.

"Not one of ours," he told us. "I was at the edge of the yard and they were all hanging over the doors watching me go."

"I thought you were going to say 'what noise?' for a minute." I don't know why I said that. It just came out.

"Why?" Ryan asked quickly.

"Because this place is a little weird."

18

"Where's the other horse, then?" Rachel asked.

"The scream came from the woods," Ryan replied. He looked totally wired.

"How come you didn't go and see?" Trust Liv to ask the wrong question. Ryan shot her a dark look.

"I thought I'd find out if you heard it too," he said defensively. But I thought I knew the truth, that he had been scared. He had just run into the house, and he still looked scared now.

"Should we all go and look now?" I suggested. "We need to make sure the horses are okay if there's a loose one around," I said, trying to make it all sound normal.

"Yes, we should, I suppose," Ryan said.

"What do you mean, 'I suppose'?" Liv asked. "It was a horse, wasn't it? We all heard it."

Ryan shrugged.

"It was," he said, "but it sounded strange out there."

"Strange how?" I asked. I glanced at Rachel, who was sharing my frown. When I turned back to Ryan he seemed to have recovered his normal composure. He started down the stairs after Liv.

"Just a little strange," he added, unhelpfully. "Kind of echoey – if you know what I mean."

"It's probably like that down in this valley," I mused, following everyone out the front door.

"We'll check the yard and take a quick look in the woods," Ryan suggested. "But any horse making that kind of sound is not sticking around." He was right. It was the

19

sound of a horse about to take flight. Luce had shown me that before.

"Where you going?" Mr. Vazquez was suddenly in the doorway behind us, holding an oven mitt.

"We'll be back in a couple of minutes," Ryan said brightly. "Just saying good-night."

We all stood there awkwardly in front of Mr. V, seeing if we'd gotten away with our white lie. There were a few seconds of total silence as he eyed us suspiciously. There wasn't a good enough reason to tell him about anything odd until we knew we had to. He'd have us packing up and leaving in an instant if he thought anything was potentially unsafe, dangerous or even unsettling for his horses.

"Dinner in fifteen minutes," he said, making eye contact with all of us before turning back to the kitchen. Ryan pulled the door open. It was still warm outside from the hot, sunny day. I was struck instantly by the total quiet of the night that surrounded us. The river was less than four yards to our right but you wouldn't even have known it was there. There was no sound coming from the water. The sense of stillness was immense, despite the crunching of our shoes on the dusty gravel. It was kind of spooky and cool, all at the same time.

"How come he didn't hear it?" Rachel whispered.

"There's an exhaust fan in the kitchen," Ryan replied, quickening his pace at the sound of a stable door being kicked. Luce, the obvious culprit, had his head over the half door, but the others soon appeared, hearing

20

our approach. Toby was the calmest, but even he wasn't happy. I went to Luce, my heart sinking at the sight of his flattened ears and anxious eyes. It was only to be expected after that terrifying sound. He was calmer within seconds of my touch.

"Was Luce okay when you left?" I asked Ryan.

"Finally," he said, from beside Red. "He was stalking around the box a little and having a good snort. He needs to get his head straight."

I felt instantly annoyed at Ryan.

"What did *he* do when you heard that horse scream?" I flashed. "What did *you* do? You ran off! He must have gone crazy, they all must have reacted – and you just ran off! No wonder he's not happy."

"I didn't run off," Ryan snapped. He was angry now but I didn't care.

"You did," Liv said, adding fuel to the fire as usual. All three of us stared at him under the dim yard lights. Ryan wasn't used to being cornered.

I looked at his handsome features, betraying the internal dilemma of how to respond to our inquisition. Luce pushed at my shoulder restlessly, breaking the tension of the standoff. I pushed back at him, waiting for Ryan to say something,

"You weren't here and you didn't hear it," he said sternly.

"What does *that* mean?" Liv said.

Rachel wasn't waiting for a full-scale argument to break out.

"Are we going to look near the woods or not?" she asked.

"*Near*?"

"Okay – you go right in there in the dark, then!"

Sometimes Ryan drove me crazy. We'd been at the location for two hours and already we were fighting. Ryan's controlled and slightly arrogant persona was mostly helpful and calming, but now he was trying to transfer his clear fright onto everyone else.

"Look," I started, "if we're not back in ten minutes we'll be in trouble." Luce nudged me, almost playful now. "He's okay, so they must be." I nodded across the yard at a disinterested Toby and the always-placid bays.

"Let's take a quick look over near the woods and go back in." I turned on my heel, not waiting for an answer. "Are you coming or not?"

I went out of the yard and turned left to go along by the river past the bridge, pleased to hear them all following me. I passed by the two tiny old two story houses, like workers cottages, which faced the river. They looked like no one had lived in them for decades. Beyond them the trail petered out into grassy scrub and became a riverside path that led off into the darkness. I was glad I wasn't heading down there – but then the woods to the left looked like an equally uninviting prospect. There was some pale moonlight outlining the tops of the tall trees. I could see that the ground rose steeply once the trees started, and the roots were growing awkwardly, grabbing at the slope like gnarled old fingers. The last time I'd seen anything like that was in a scary film that I'd watched with my dad about a mad horseman. It wasn't an image I wanted popping into my head at that moment. Ryan was suddenly next to me and I jumped.

We waited a moment and then crossed the remaining tufted summer grass, slowly – like hunters stalking prey.

I stopped at the first tree and listened. The grass gave way to dusty soil as the woods began. An owl hooted in the distance as I made a step up the slope. There was no way I was venturing into the blackness beyond, with the tree roots twisting all around, looking like they were waiting to trip you up or make a grab at your ankle. There is nothing scarier than woods in the darkness, and just to prove the point we heard one of those night rustlings from within the trees. I was used to them from home, but in this place, with those creepy roots … I took a step backwards. There was no horse in there, and if there was, I felt sorry for the beast.

"I don't *like* this," I heard Liv say, in a nervous, singsong voice.

"There's nothing there. Come on," Rachel said urgently. "Let's go in."

I turned, waiting for Ryan to say something contrary. He didn't and we walked back to the farmhouse.

The atmosphere at supper was subdued. Mr. Vazquez had made his special pasta and tomato sauce from ingredients he'd picked up from the market before we got onto the ferry. He was a really good chef and took the same amount of time over the preparation and cooking as he did with his horses. The result was always so nice, but because of what had happened beforehand it didn't taste quite as good as usual.

I noticed Ryan eyeing me from across the broad wooden table in the middle of the large kitchen, probably deciding how moody he was going to be with me later because we'd argued in the yard. I guess I'd fought him a little too hard. It was just further proof that I'd protect my horse no matter what – even against a throwaway comment from Ryan, whom I'd pretty much die for too! I guess I loved Luce more than anything, ever. I got the feeling, though, that we were all on edge. I hadn't really felt right since Luce had come charging down the ramp looking like he was trying to escape a pack of demons. Then there was the old man watching us. I had a funny feeling and I couldn't shake it off.

I decided to talk to Ryan later and tell him I was sorry. I didn't want to mess up the whole trip by having a simmering argument with him – on top of worrying about the vaulting I had to perform. Ryan could keep up a moody act for days.

When I zoned back into the conversation at the table, Mr. Vazquez was giving us a kind of briefing.

"We have two full days to prepare and then two full days shooting the fairground scenes and maybe one more for re-shooting if they need."

"They're editing on site, aren't they?" Ryan asked.

Mr. Vazquez nodded. "Yes, so we will know if they have what they need."

"How many actors will there be?" Liv asked.

"There will be two hundred extras on the three days of filming and the two principal actors.

"Just for a flashback sequence? How funny!"

"Have you read the script?" Rachel asked her, suddenly animated. "It's a crucial flashback sequence in the movie. The grown-up girl character keeps having this memory of going to the fair as a child and something is given to her by a stranger while she's there. Every time they do the flashback in the film you see a little bit more. I really want to see this when it's finished. It's a great story!"

"And who showed you the script?"

The smile vanished from Rachel's face as she turned and attempted to answer her father's question.

"Uh. It was … on … your ... desk."

Liv and I started to giggle as Rachel looked suitably mortified. "Sorry," she said to her dad. Even I knew the rules about poking around Mr. Vazquez's desk trying to find stuff out about the projects.

Mr. Vazquez looked at Rachel for about five seconds. He was at his most scary when he said nothing. We waited for him to dish some sort of punishment out to Rachel, but instead he stood and began clearing the plates.

"What about the actress we'll be working with?" I asked. "Hayley something? I heard she's playing her own mother in the scenes?"

"Have you read the script too?" Ryan asked me.

"*You* told me." I replied quickly … and then wished I hadn't. Ryan had clearly been doing a whole load of snooping around his dad's desk too.

Mr. Vazquez looked at his son, who shot me an evil look across the table.

"Actually, it wasn't you, it was Rach." I convinced myself, but not Mr. Vazquez. He looked at me like I was a total idiot. I decided to keep my mouth shut for the rest of the evening as I felt Rachel's elbow dig into my side.

I muttered "Sorry," and wished for my bed and tomorrow.

Sleep didn't come easily. I heard the other two drift off. Rachel hadn't been in a bad mood, even after I'd gotten her in trouble again in my attempt to get Ryan off the hook. She never got in a bad mood with anyone. We lay in bed laughing at her mouthing off about the script. It felt good to do that rather than remember the sound of the stray horse and the horrible woods. But it was the knotted tree roots that I lay there thinking about as I tried to get to sleep. And just as I had the idea to sneak across the landing and smooth things over with Ryan I must have nodded off, because the next thing I knew it was morning. The sun was peeking through the curtains and the birds were singing.

"Look at the time! Get up, you two, before we're in more trouble!"

Liv burst in from the bathroom, clutching a towel around herself. I looked at my alarm clock. It was 8:30!

Liv began fiddling with her eyeliner at the mirror.

"Ry's down in the yard with your dad and they've done everything. We're sooo dead!"

Rachel groaned and put her head under the comforter.

"I may as well stay here all day," she said. "Everything I do is bound to be wrong. Why didn't they just wake us up?"

"It was a test and we failed," Liv offered. Her eyes lit up. "We could say we're all sick," she suggested.

I looked at her as if she was mental and shook my head. Anyway, I wanted to go and see Luce and make the most of the day.

"It's these beds. They're too comfortable!" Liv said. She was right about that. I'd slept like a log once I'd finally dropped off.

We were all down in the yard fifteen minutes later. Mr. Vazquez ignored us as he returned the rakes to the little shed. The horses were all out in the field that stretched away up the hill behind the yard. Everything was done.

"Well done, idiots," Ryan said under his breath. Liv opened her mouth to respond but Mr. Vazquez's voice boomed across the flagstones before she could speak. I saw Liv flinch as if she'd been hit in the head with a brick, and despite the situation I laughed out loud. It was all too stupid.

"Inside," came the command.

We filed into the kitchen after him and sat around the

table in silence. I felt my mouth wanting to laugh and willed myself not to catch Liv or Rachel's eye.

"No more sleeping late. No more fighting. No more lying," was all Mr. Vazquez said. Far less scary than I thought he'd be.

We nodded.

"Can we go for a ride?" I wanted to be with Luce.

"You all have a good breakfast and go. Back here at noon."

We all nodded again. Liv stood up quickly and knocked her chair over backwards. I squeezed my eyes closed to stop a giggle.

"I'll cut some bread," she said.

Mr. Vazquez watched her for a moment.

"Ryan, you come with me," he said. They left by the back door and Mr. Vazquez closed it firmly behind him. The three of us sat down again.

"Let's just have breakfast and go for a ride," I suggested.

"Yeah, lets." Rachel agreed.

Half an hour later we were tacking up in the yard.

"I know where they've gone," Liv stood with her hands on her hips. "To the set. They knew we'd want to go there, so they've gone off without us. That's our punishment."

"It's my fault for blabbing that I'd read the script," Rachel said.

"That was just the start, though. We totally annoyed

him and then we all overslept," I sighed. "We were bound to get in trouble."

"We won't miss anything, you know," Liv said defiantly. "There are no background artists there today. They'll just be setting up and checking to make sure everything's okay. Your dad will be checking to see if the vaulting circle is the right size – things like that. Boring! I hope Ryan is bored, bored, bored," she laughed. "He must have done some major sucking up this morning to get himself completely out of trouble. Well done, Ry!"

Liv clapped sarcastically. "And I won't forgive him for not waking us up."

Agreeing with everything she had said, I grinned. Ryan didn't often get into trouble with Mr. Vazquez, but when he did, he made sure he did everything he could to get himself out of it.

"Let's go for a ride and then start practicing in the field." I suggested. My friends nodded and we made for the back door.

I felt a knot of nerves as I went over to Luce. He tossed his head and snorted impatiently, then kicked the door.

"Hey" I scolded. "We'll have none of that!" I wagged my finger at him. He stared back at me defiantly, but as always with an underlying softness. I turned to Rachel.

"He's okay. We can follow the path up under the trees."

It was just beginning to feel warm as we rode side-by-side-by-side up the hill away from the farm. The edge of the woods was always to our right and we soon passed the point where I had seen the old man watching us. I could feel the tension in my horse's muscles as we reached the top of the slope. Before us was a grassy plateau ringed by the woods to the right. It was like the top of a hill had been sliced off, leaving a large flat top.

"This is nice," Rachel said, halting beside me on her sweet bay Velvet, as I battled to keep Luce still. Liv cantered ahead on Chokky to the far edge of the space and then came back. Chokky halted beautifully in front of us in a way only highly trained horses can, with a rider they totally trust. Liv and Chokky had developed a fantastic intuition.

"There's a little hill and then open field. Want to go for a gallop?"

Luce was raring to go. He lurched to the right as if he was making a break for the trees around the clearing.

"What is it with you and trees!" I said lightly. But he really, really wanted to go. What had been nerves in the yard now seemed to be utter compulsion to head for the woods. Liv and Rachel started at a gallop across the plateau and I managed to get Luce to follow them. We stopped at the top of the hill before taking the slope cautiously and then galloping again, hooves pounding the peaty earth, happily distracted as we enjoyed the exhilaration of our full flight, our hair flying behind us, delight on our faces. It was fantastic, exploring new places and giving the horses their first good exercise since the long journey.

We continued across the vast space. The grass was growing close to the ground and there was nothing except a few patches of scrubby brush, and a couple of mounds with long grasses growing around them. Right in the distance I could see the hazy horizon made up of two shades of blue.

"The sea!" I shouted.

We reined in perfectly in unison.

"So nice!" Rachel said happily. "There really is nothing here, is there? I love it!"

I turned Luce and we looked back across the huge space. He snorted and charged a few steps, eager to do the return gallop. Down here, away from the trees, he seemed completely content.

"Race you back!"

Chokky surged ahead, the lightest and most nimble of the three. Luce gained on them gradually, his Lusitano powers of acceleration in full swing. I whooped as we passed, laughing as we reined in at the base of the slope a few minutes later.

"Next time," Liv said breathlessly, as she always did, knowing they could never win.

We spent a while longer on the open field. I wanted to stay, knowing Luce seemed at ease. I hoped he would shake off whatever was interfering with his good behavior. We took the hill at a gallop on the way back. My heart sank because, as anticipated, as soon as we were back on the plateau I felt him tense up. I ignored it until suddenly he swayed dramatically to the left and made a dart for the woods once again.

I squeezed the reins and kept my weight well into the saddle. He slowed and I saw the opportunity to turn him to face the other two.

"What's his game?" Liv said. "You silly boy!"

I grimaced as he tried to turn back, more half-hearted than before.

"He wants to go into the woods." I said, shaking my head.

"Do you think?"

"Definitely. He was fine out in the field and he's kind of fine in the stable." I laughed. I wasn't finding it funny, though. He absolutely *had* to behave.

"You need to work this out," Liv said.

I rolled my eyes, still struggling with my horse's determination to head to the left.

"Can you two get on this side of me?" I asked the girls. Liv and Chokky rallied to my left, placing themselves between the trees and us.

"Walk!" I commanded sternly and we headed for the grassy path beside the field. As we reached the top of the hill Luce started to relax and I was able to let my guard down, but then I looked up and felt a shudder of fright. The old man was there again, under the trees, overlooking the field in exactly the same place he had been the evening before.

Chapter 3

It was as though he was waiting for us. He looked up from his slightly stooped position as he spoke.

"Good day to you," the man said. His voice was clear and strong.

"Hello," Rachel replied. "Do you live around here?"

He nodded. "Not far."

"Where?" Rachel asked, "We didn't see any …"

"Don't go into them woods up there."

I swallowed as the suddenly stern words reached my ears. The three of us stared at him.

"Why?"

He didn't reply. He looked like he didn't have an answer.

"We heard a loose horse last night," Liv said. "Was it your horse?"

The man shook his head. "Don't know what you mean," he replied.

Luce seemed to have had enough and I let him walk on down the slope and heard the others following.

"Thanks. We probably will stay out of the woods." Rachel said, and at that moment I really agreed with her. Luce acting strangely. Scary old man with a warning. Screaming stray horses. All I wanted to do was focus on the filming and stay out of trouble. I didn't want anything freaking me out on this trip. But things were happening already.

I could see Ryan and Mr. Vazquez down in the yard as we descended the slope.

Liv glanced over her shoulder.

"He's gone," she said. "Do you think he hung around just to tell us that?"

"He was scary," Rachel said. "He was freaking Velvet out."

"Me too," Liv added. "Especially with Luce acting up and wanting to do exactly what he was telling us not to do!"

"I know," I sighed. "He said 'the woods up there', didn't he? As in, right where Luce wanted to go into the trees."

"Maybe the man has something to hide?" Liv suggested. "Maybe he lives in there and he doesn't want us poking around."

"Why? Is he running some kind of illegal operation and we've showed up so he's trying to scare us off?"

"Maybe." Liv chuckled.

"I don't think so somehow," I said.

Liv turned to me. "How can you be sure?"

"He looked about seventy five and he can't even stand up straight!" I laughed. "So unless we're part of some crazy film plot a bit different from the kind of script you took an illegal peek at, Rach, no eighty-year-old criminal mastermind is hiding out the middle of the woods."

"So why the warning?" Rachel came alongside as we reached the yard.

"I don't know," I told her. But somehow, I thought we were going to find out, whether we liked it or not.

Mr. Vazquez wasn't totally ignoring us, but we kept a low profile watering, grooming and picking out hooves before turning the horses out into the field. Luce had almost been okay in the yard. I watched now as he turned away from me dramatically and raced to the top of the hill, his thick mane and tail rippling like silky waves as he went. I grimaced as he gained the brow of the hill, half expecting him to take the fence at the top and head off for the woods. Thankfully, he stopped at the top of the ridge, turned sideways, tossed his head back and whinnied. I shook my head and headed in for some lunch.

Ryan told us all about the set over the meal. He was pretending to be informative, but we all knew he was being smug. Liv was interjecting with an occasional "*really*!" and a fake wide-eyed expression of interest. She finished with,

"Thanks *so* much for telling us all about it.' She gave Ryan a sickly smile that lasted half a second and then stole a quick glance at Mr. Vazquez to see if she had gotten away with it. He was slicing garlic as thin as paper for some supper dish he was preparing and hadn't been listening to us.

"It's nearly all set up anyway," Ryan continued. "Maybe you'll see it tomorrow … if you keep your mouths shut and set your alarms."

I heard Mr. Vazquez's 'Heh, heh' laugh from over by the sink. Ryan joined in with a burst of laughter himself. Liv flailed an arm out behind her and smashed her fist into the cupboard instead of Ryan's leg. Mr. Vazquez turned sharply. Liv tried to look normal as she shook out the pain. I thought it was a good idea to leave just then to run through my vaulting.

We got started and Rachel ran through her movements effortlessly, looking happy. With Liv holding the rope, she sailed past me doing her Basic Seat, arms out to her sides, hands at ear level – her ponytail bouncing as Velvet cantered on, with the barest contact with the rope. Next she moved on to a Flag, hopping onto her knees and extending her right leg out slightly above her head. She followed it with an effortless Mill, her legs moving like a gymnast as she completed a full turn around the horse, in four stages.

Rachel had been vaulting for three years, and Liv too. They were both terrific at it and could do all the exercises.

They were also terrific lungers. Lunger is the name of the person in the middle of a circle, who is in charge of controlling the speed of the horse on a lunge line with a deft touch of the whip. For the shoot, because we were supposed to look like country girls providing a bit of entertainment, we weren't going to do any of the more complex moves. We were going to be wearing dresses, for one, so there wouldn't be any of the upside down exercises! We'd be leaving that to Ryan.

I looked at Luce as he shook his head and stamped the ground. All of a sudden, I knew these fun, simple exercises were beyond us. We weren't as experienced as the other two, but back home in the field, you wouldn't really have noticed. I knew that Luce was not happy here, in this weird place, and so I wasn't either.

I rose too slowly for my Flag, and I didn't get my weight right, with too much on the front of my foot, and Luce felt the pressure and jerked sideways. I took another pass, trying to feel good as the warm air brushed past my face and we did better, but there was no way I could do it smiling and laughing like Liv and Rachel had been doing.

"Relax, Salma," Rachel called. They had obviously been watching me closely, taking in my lack of confidence.

"Something's not right with him." I called. "He's making me nervous."

I stopped.

Rachel shook her head. "You can't let that happen," she said.

Liv shrugged. "He's acting weird – so what's new!" she said. I knew she was trying to lighten my mood.

Luce snorted perfectly on cue.

"He knows you're not happy and he's feeding off that, which is making him worse. We're not supposed to do this like we're in competition, anyway. It's supposed to be relaxed and fun looking – not too precise."

Rachel nodded. "You should have seen your face on that first Flag."

I sighed and thought for a moment, burying the slightly indignant feeling I had at their joint criticism. They were right, though, and they were trying to help me, but I would always be miles behind them in terms of experience. Compared to them I was practically a beginner. These horses didn't *do* nervous riders. That's why we were paid to come and ride them. The actors hardly ever got to ride one of our boys, not unless they had a couple of weeks to build up the trust.

"It's hard when he just wants to go into the woods!"

"Forget about the woods and pretend we're at home," Rachel said. "You know you're not going to fall off."

"Why are we even doing vaulting when it probably wasn't even invented when the film is set?" I said irritably.

"You sound like me!" Liv shouted. "Get on with it and show him who's boss. I know I'm controlling him, but all he's interested in is you."

I shook the confused thoughts from my head and gave Luce a pat. The next time around it all felt better; not

terrific, just better – and it was a start. I even managed
a spontaneous smile as we finished our Mill. It was the
hardest vault we'd have to do, where you basically move
your body in a circle around the horse's saddle in four
movements.

"See?" Liv called. So I went again just to prove it.

Back in the yard I felt like I'd finished a dreaded exam and
done okay. Luce might not be totally happy but if he knew
I wasn't then everything would fall apart. I had to keep my
nerves in check. Rachel and Liv were right. If I could find
out what was bothering him, it would be a start.

I talked to Luce as I groomed him. I could tell he didn't
want to be back in the yard at all. I doubted he was eager
to get back into the field and practice again, either. He
wasn't much of a fan of the special roller and back pad he
had to wear for the vaulting.

It was getting late when Ryan and Mr. Vazquez
returned. We had started our evening routine after a couple
of hours sitting by the river, followed by some time in
the room playing around with Liv's hair straighteners. I
didn't use them. I liked my wavy hair, but Liv ironed hers
flat and we all fooled around with some new silver eye
shadow in a tiny pot. It looked amazing on Rachel, a little
crazy on Liv with her light blue eyes, and weird on me but
kind of cool because I had put it on with my finger and
didn't blend it in.

✳   ✳   ✳   ✳

39

Ryan dismounted next to me as Red greeted his buddy Luce. It wasn't often they were apart. I loved it when I looked out onto our field in the mornings and saw them, always together, apart from the other three.

"Interested in a quick ride?" Ryan asked me, frowning slightly at my silvery eyes. He nodded at Luce. "He is."

I laughed and mounted bareback. "I'll show you what's up there." I pointed up the hill.

We walked up the grassy path beneath the trees. I was relieved to see there was no scary old man waiting at the top of the hill. It reminded me to tell Ryan what he had said to us that morning.

"Was he where he was the night before?"

I nodded. "Almost exactly. It's like he just steps out of the woods."

"There're no houses in there, though, are there?"

"Doubt it," I shrugged. "I don't really feel like checking."

The daylight was fading away. I didn't want us to be out for long.

"We could go for a ride around the outside – see if there are any roads going in. People do live in woods you know."

I laughed. Both of our houses are in dense woods.

"Weird people like you." I told him

"Who live opposite even weirder people," he countered.

I looked across at him and saw half a smile as he turned away from me to look ahead. We had reached the brow of the hill at the top of the horses' field and there was the flat

40

open space ahead of us. Just at that moment Luce veered sharply to the right. I pulled him back but he wanted to head for the trees just as he had done earlier. Ryan was frowning as I turned back to him.

"He did that a couple of times earlier."

Luce pranced again and shimmied backwards. I struggled to keep him facing away from the trees, figuring that was the best course of action.

"He wants to go into the woods, and has since he came out of the trailer." Finally he stood still.

"Maybe it's not such a good idea to ride around the outside of the woods," Ryan said. He thought for a moment. "But going straight through them isn't such a great idea either," he said. "Come on. We'll go around – do what we said we were going to do – and he can just behave."

Ryan rode ahead to the crest of the hill, overlooking the fields.

"Easier said than done," I murmured, as we followed.

It was a battle to catch up with them, with Luce constantly wanting to go to the right. Eventually I was beside Ryan and Red and we negotiated the gentle slope, bearing right to hug the contour of the woods as they skirted the base of the hill. Luce was walking like he was on hot coals, but now at least I felt in charge. The woods seemed to take the shape of an upturned bowl. We followed the rim around to the right. It took ten minutes to get roughly halfway around, and by then Luce had completely calmed down. I thought we might be learning

41

something about his strange anxiety. We went uphill slightly, at the furthest point from the farmhouse, and then it was a gentle slope down to the river. We turned back along the dusty narrow trail that led along the bank and back to the farm.

Just before we reached the stables we once again turned back up the hill, along a narrow cut-through down the back of the barn and on up the hill next to the field.

Ryan was watching Luce, and at that moment I felt his muscles begin to tense up. Something clicked in my head.

"He's been fine since we went down the hill from the plateau," Ryan said.

"It's not the woods," I said. "It's just that part of them, up there ... I think."

Ryan was staring at me as if I was crazy.

"And why would that be?" he said slowly. Part of me wanted to tell him to get lost, but another argument right now wasn't the best option. Plus, I could see a hint of humor in his face. He liked to joke about my strange horse. I paused for a moment longer before telling him my theory.

"He wants to go into the woods ... up there ... to a certain part of them. The part the old man warned us about." I nodded in the direction of the brow of the hill. "It's when we get up there to the clearing that he starts acting up."

Ryan stared at Luce as if he was expecting some horse input.

"Shall we go and find out exactly how insane your horse is?" he sighed.

I looked around. Darkness was drawing ever closer.

"Yes," I replied, pushing Luce on up the hill. "Let's do it."

We walked the horses up the hill. Halfway up Luce lurched forward and I let him go, which he wasn't expecting. We crested the hill and he headed without hesitation across the open space to the right, toward the trees that bordered the space. Luce's gallop petered out for a moment as Ryan and Red came alongside. He shook his mane out and stamped the earth, still surprised that I was letting him do pretty much what he wanted. He threw his head back theatrically and let out a whinny and then broke into a gallop toward the center of the tree line. We were still at full speed ten yards away and all I could see was a wall of trees. I decided to take control and we stopped. The woods here were made up of mature chestnut trees, with their strange branches hanging down like the finger bones on a skeleton. I could make out the occasional unusually tall oak tree in between and a few sparse looking bushes and saplings – spindly and starved of light. It was too dark to see very far in. As we stood there I felt that eerie quiet that settles over woods – an air of mystery hanging in the branches and the leaves.

Luce stared ahead and stamped the ground. I leaned over and patted and stroked his neck.

"Show us, then," I said to him softly, and immediately he walked on in between the first two trees.

Ryan and Red followed. I ducked and pushed aside the lowest hanging branches. Luce seemed to know exactly where he was going and I felt uneasy knowing that the clearing was now a good way behind us. All four of us were suddenly enveloped by the trees. It felt as if we were at the center of the thickest forest. Luce weaved through the trunks as we walked on in silence. I knew he could see far better than we could through the gloom. Just when I was about to call out a halt to our roaming, the trees seemed to thin out slightly. There were no really big trees, but a few smaller ones. There had once been a huge one a little way ahead; we could see that right away. Now it was just a trunk extending only a few yards up, ending in jagged shapes, the edges smoothed over time by the elements.

The light was fading seriously fast now. Great, I thought as Luce moved forwards.

"Great," Ryan said sarcastically. "He found a dead tree."

I laughed, needing to break the tension. Luce was calm, staring ahead. For the first time since the ferry, I had my horse back.

"Very interesting. Thanks, Luce," Ryan said.

Luce remained steadfast.

"We should at least do him the honor of poking around a little," I said, dismounting. Ryan reluctantly joined me on the uneven ground. I looked around, knowing it was the last few moments of daylight.

"Maybe we should come back another time?"

"We may as well have a quick look," Ryan said. He

began trampling over the spiny little trees and brushed past the lower branches of the larger ones. I did the same and turned back to the two horses, who waited side by side.

"You could at least give us a clue, you crazy fool!" Ryan called over his shoulder.

"Is there treasure here maybe, a trapdoor ... leading to a labyrinth? The holy grail?" he laughed.

We walked on over the lumpy ground.

"Well, I'm not about to excavate the place." Ryan muttered. "We could be here for hours looking for whatever *he* wants us to find."

He took another step forwards, toward the huge jagged tree stump – and the next thing I saw were his arms flailing in the air as he slid downwards and out of my sight.

I hurried forwards, concentrating on the ground and careful of my step. With relief I saw Ryan lying down in a hole, starting to stand up. He was at least two yards below me and appeared to have fallen down into some sort of well-hidden pit.

"You okay?"

The dusk was playing with my vision and his outline appeared grainy. But now I could see he was standing.

"Think so," he called up. "What is this place?"

A rumble of thunder reached my ears and I felt the need to get out of the woods altogether. I suddenly knew that there was a secret here. And I knew that it wasn't a nice one. Ryan turned to make his way back up to me and immediately stumbled. He turned and scowled down at whatever had caused him to trip. I watched him bend down and begin to push various pieces of woodland debris aside. He crouched, peering closer, frowning …

Ryan pulled at something. He looked again and then tugged with more force.

"Salma, come here."

Easier said than done. I scrambled down the steep slope into the pit, fear and adrenalin surging through me. Ryan started clawing at the earth, and then he stood and pulled at the object again, nearly flying backwards as it came loose in his hand. I saw what it was immediately, with a mixture of horror and amazement.

I reached for my phone, remembering the flashlight gadget it had on it. I had laughed when I first saw the feature, wondering when it would ever need to be used. I pointed the beam of white light along what Ryan had unearthed and we looked at each other.

"It's a bone."

Now even Ryan was sounding unnerved. He ran his hand along its smooth white length. It was about half a yard long. Complete. It was unmistakably a bone, with a slightly odd looking shape, flaring out at the top. It was both terrifying and beautiful.

"It looks like a leg bone," I whispered.

Ryan nodded. "It is," he said grimly.

"Must be a man to be that size?" I ventured.

He shook his head. "It's not human," he said.

He turned and stared at me.

"It's from a horse."

My whole body shook as the deafening equine scream erupted around us once again. An echo from everywhere and nowhere. It was not Luce or Red.

The next thing we heard was Luce's own scream piercing the gloom. I turned just in time to see the flick of his back hooves as he took off through the woods.

Chapter 4

We scrambled out of the pit to where both horses had been standing. Red thought about going, but miraculously he had stayed put. We reached him just as he was about to take off. Ryan held his nose and pressed his face into Red's flanks. I watched them. Even in this moment of mayhem the sight of Ryan and Red together like that in the near dark touched my heart.

"I'm going after Luce."

I picked my way out, dodging through the trees, feeling instantly alone just a few yards from where I had left Ryan and Red. I tried to run as straight as possible, fixing a point ahead and weaving my way past the thick trunks. The problem was, I wasn't sure that I had picked the right point ahead when I had started moving. Although I was careful not to fall, it was impossible not to stumble almost every other step on the saplings and dead branches strewn over the floor of the woods. I kept going, feeling a rising panic as it dawned on me that I should have made it out into the clearing by now. But there was no sight of it, and the darkness was making it even more difficult to see a way through and out.

I stopped and listened, long enough to hear a few dreaded woodland rustlings. Then I made another mistake. I turned and looked back at where I had come from and considered retracing my steps. I shook my head and turned back the way I had been going, or the way I *thought* I had been going, mad at myself for not getting my bearings right in the first place. I felt like I was playing that childhood party game, where you are blindfolded and spun around in the center of a circle and you head forwards and try and work out who is in front of you. Now I didn't really know which way I was facing and I wasn't sure which direction was even vaguely *out*. "What a total idiot." I said aloud. The trees seemed to be closing in on me from all sides and I felt my eyes widen in fear.

"Ry!" I called out.

No answer came. I stumbled blindly forwards, hoping I could get myself somewhere near the edge of the woods. If Ryan had gotten out and not found me or Luce he would have gone back to the farm, assuming that was where we both were, and I would be left alone in the horrible woods, with their bones and heaven knows what else. Stopping was a bad idea because the little sounds that broke the blanket of silence started freaking me out even more.

Then I knew I was not alone. There was a rustling, coming closer. A twig snapped. Something was coming toward me. I sank down next to a huge oak trunk and huddled myself into a ball. I was trapped in my worst nightmare.

Luce's gentle whinny made my heart skip a few beats. Then he was there, beside me, nudging my elbow. I stood and vaulted onto his back, unable to do anything except lie low on his neck and bury my face into his mane as he walked calmly out of the woods into the clearing where Ryan and Red were waiting for us. Ryan looked very relieved.

"He went in to get you," he told me, turning Red and falling in beside us.

"I'm not sure I can talk for a moment," I replied.

Ryan nodded and we walked on in silence while I took some deep breaths. I could hardly believe I was out of the woods and reunited with my horse.

I stood in the yard with Luce, hugging him and resting my cheek on his nose.

"What happened to you?" Ryan said, as we were ready to go in.

"I got lost. I must have headed off slightly in the wrong direction and gone parallel to the clearing. I shouted but I don't think you heard me."

Ryan shook his head. "No, we didn't," he told me, "but he might have," Ryan gestured at Luce.

"Where was he when you got out?"

"Just a short way into the clearing, waiting. We saw you weren't there and waited for a while longer. Then he just trotted off and found you. He knew exactly where to go." Ryan gave a little laugh through his nose. "Didn't you? Weirdo!"

Ryan called over his shoulder at the sultry black face, watching us intently over the half door. I wanted to go back to him, but we'd had enough fussing and hugs for one evening.

As we all lay in bed, I told the girls about the woods, glossing over the part about being lost in the trees because I didn't want to recount it in too much detail for my own sanity! Mr. Vazquez was on the phone to the police down in the hall, his brief conversation drifting up the stairs. He thought someone should know about the horse bone. I thought so too, considering the old man had tried to warn us away from that part of the woods. We realized that none of us had set an alarm again, and after a flurry of activity I was back under the covers and fell asleep as soon as my head hit the pillow.

"There she is!" Liv was pointing in a really obvious way across the set to the big black SUV that had pulled up on the far side at the security gate.

51

"Be cool!" I said, laughing and dragging her arm downwards.

We watched as the young actress was greeted by the Director and his assistant. She was tiny, with very long, wavy brown hair. There were other important and slightly scary looking people standing around, a couple of them in suits. Thankfully we didn't have to bother with them much. We'd be hearing the word "action" and doing our thing.

The set was fantastic. They had created a perfect old-fashioned country showground. Around the outside of the field was a ring of gypsy-looking wooden caravans, painted with pretty flowers and carved with curvy edges. There were trestle tables of stalls being set up too and a lot of busy carpenters milling around.

We all stood there with the horses, ready to talk things through with the Director and get a feel for the space. We were inside a ring of straw bales where our display would be taking place in front of the crowd. We were the background artists. The flashback scene that Rachel already knew all about would happen in front of us. We just had to keep our display going as the cameras rolled on the important little scene of a small child with her mother at the fair. The actress, Hayley Watts, was playing the teenage girl in the present day, but in the flashback scenes, set fifteen years earlier, she was also playing her own mother.

We had done a run-through and asked for the ring to be made even bigger. Mr. Vazquez and the Assistant Director

Mike had adjusted our starting position and been spraying the grass with marks. Mr. Vazquez was our lunger. Ryan was going to ride both Red and Toby. Although Red was a superb stunt horse and well trained in vaulting there were a couple of things that Ryan could do on Toby that would never go wrong.

Ryan went into the ring and did a full set of vaults. Although we had stopped at a Mill, Ryan went on to Scissors, landing softly on Toby's back. Then he went on to a Stand, and finally a Flank, the last and most difficult of the modern vaulting movements involving a handstand followed by Ryan swinging his whole body on either side of Toby. I felt a surge of pride as I watched and a few people clapped as he finished and dismounted perfectly.

I felt as if I truly had my horse back. Luce was calm today and enjoying the bustle. I got back up in the saddle to make sure that his impeccable behavior earlier hadn't been a fluke. I did another set of three vaults and it felt great. There could be no nerves tomorrow, when all the extras would be watching and the cameras would be rolling. I sat back down on his broad back and a round of applause rang out. I turned and smiled back at the people who had turned to watch and were showing their appreciation. I felt myself blush, half wishing they weren't watching, and half pleased that it was giving me a taste of what things would be like the day after.

There was a newcomer to our huddle. Hayley Watts. I walked back over slowly, watching the early interaction.

Hayley was about Rachel's age, so just a little older than me. She really was dazzlingly pretty with small, neat features, green eyes and perfect skin. And of course, to whom was she giving all her attention – already, after, like two minutes? Ryan.

I didn't need to go over and hear what she was saying because she was pretty loud.

"Are these guys your horses?" she asked.

No, I thought. We rent them.

They watched me approach and everyone applauded again as I dismounted.

"Salma, this is Hayley," Liv said, a slightly insincere look on her face.

I'd seen Hayley in a magazine on the ferry, dressed in a white gown on a red carpet somewhere. She was even prettier in real life.

"Hi!" she said. "That was great!"

"Thanks," I smiled.

"I love him," she nodded at Luce. He snorted and nodded his head. "Hah! So *cool*."

Liv was eyeing her with suspicion, as I could have predicted. She was always like that with new, smiley, enthusiastic people. Ryan had started smiling back at Hayley. Great. My heart sank.

"I just had to come right over," she said, laughing and touching Ryan's arm. Three minutes was all she had been with us. The rule was proven once and for all. There was no one who didn't like Ryan.

Hayley got called over by Mike.

"Surprised she didn't ask you out," Liv quipped.

"Oh, shut up," Ryan snapped. "She was just being friendly and nice. Do you know what those words mean?"

He stalked off back to Red.

"At least she was nice," Rachel said. "Better than some we've known. Remember that witch on the last shoot?"

We laughed. Ryan turned and gave us a dirty look.

"Not laughing at you, Ry," I called. He looked away.

"Not yet," Liv shouted.

I shook my head, but I couldn't help laughing. Ryan gave Liv a disgusted look as we mounted up, ready for a nice fifteen-minute ride back to the farm.

There was a police car waiting outside the farmhouse when we crossed the bridge. I was puzzled for a moment by the sight of it, but then I quickly remembered the events of the evening before. Thanks to the bustle of the set, unearthed bones seemed another world away. The car's two occupants got out as we approached the yard. The older, larger of the two held up an ID card.

Mr. Vazquez dismounted and spoke to them. I watched, and couldn't help noticing that the other, younger policeman was very nice looking.

"Ryan and Salma," Mr. Vazquez called to us.

We dismounted and passed the reins to Rachel and Liv. The older policeman looked like something out of a TV series, with his slightly craggy, friendly face.

"We've come to talk to you about the discovery you made in the woods last night. I'm Detective Peterson and this is Detective Morgan." He nodded to his fair haired, boyish looking companion. "We'd like you to show us the remains if you can,"

Ryan nodded. "I can show you," he said.

I wanted to go back to the woods in the daytime so I'd see them in their relatively un-scary state. "I'll come too," I said.

"We'll take our horses," Ryan told them. "That way we can show you how we found the place – or how Salma's horse found it."

Ryan grinned, a little embarrassed. I guessed he hadn't meant to reveal that part of the proceedings.

"Lead the way," Peterson gestured. "We'll be glad to walk. Anything to get away from that car on a hot day,"

We led them up the hill and across the clearing and stood once again facing the line of trees. Luce was relaxed but, unbelievably, he seemed to know our purpose.

"He's got a bit of a sixth sense," I told the detectives, hoping they wouldn't think I was too crazy. "He just took us to this pit in the middle of the woods. He seemed to want us to find it." I shrugged awkwardly.

Peterson nodded and Morgan smiled. "Has he shown psychic ability before?" he asked.

Ryan and I looked at each other. "Yes," we replied together.

The policemen chuckled. "Maybe we could use him," Peterson said. "Will you be able to show us again now?"

"We can try," Ryan said. "I dropped the bone trying to reach my horse before he took off. I hope it's still there. We both saw it, didn't we?"

I nodded at the police as Ryan went on, "But maybe Luce and Red should stay out here, and I can try to find the dead tree."

I decided to give Luce a green light and he walked forwards calmly. He was showing us again. The others followed as he led us back into the trees. Luce snorted a little and I felt him tense up, his ears flicking back dangerously. We pressed on and a minute or so later we were standing over the pit, staring across at the dead tree. Ryan dismounted and looked at Luce with concern.

"Right. I think he should get out of here," he said. "This is definitely the right place. It was just down there where I found the bone," Ryan pointed to below our feet.

"Do you want to take them both back?" he said to me.

I did and I nodded, taking Red's reins as Ryan led the detectives down into the hole.

I decided I might as well go back to the farmhouse. We crossed the clearing, and then a surprise I didn't want was waiting around the corner.

The old man was there again, at the top of the slope overlooking the field.

Luce reared, and luckily Red half joined him so I managed to keep hold of both of them and stay up.

"More visitors," he said.

"The police," I replied, without thinking, battling with two horses who were trying to spin and bounce in two directions. "We found something in the woods."

The man looked suddenly distressed, and I didn't want to talk to him any more.

"What did you find?" he rasped, taking a step toward me.

Luce and Red were on high alert, but then the man seemed to calm down.

"*He* knew there was something there." The old man nodded at Luce. "Those woods are cursed. Cursed, they are. I'm telling you ..." His voice drifted off on the breeze.

"Do you know what happened in the woods?" I asked cautiously. "Why are they cursed?"

He shook his head slowly.

"Was it something to do with that horse we heard?"

The man continued shaking his head. "I knew there was something there ..." his voice drifted off. Had he been warning us based on some kind of a hunch? It would explain why he hadn't told us anything solid.

"Those young neighbors will be over to see you," he said, suddenly smiling brightly, as if someone had flicked a switch.

"Nice boy and his sister. Fern and Edward, their names are."

I was glad he had changed the subject, but I wasn't really listening to him. I doubted there were any "neighbors."

I smiled back kindly. "We'll look out for them." I said, finally having control of Red and Luce. I called "Bye" and kept going down the hill.

Ryan wasn't far behind me. Morgan and Peterson were on their cell phones in the yard. Apparently there was a strong signal because of the number of people who worked at the power station. Ryan came in through the back door looking wired.

"What?" we all asked at once.

He blew out a stream of air.

"Where's Dad?" he asked.

"He'll be down in a minute," Rachel replied.

Ryan sat down at the kitchen table and ran his hands through his hair.

"Did you find the bone again?"

He nodded. "And then another bone, and another, pretty much strewn everywhere, half buried, most of them, and caught in the ivy. Once we found the one from yesterday they asked me to wait at the edge of the pit. They were so careful, brushing the ivy aside. Not like us yesterday, blundering around the place like elephants. It was like no one had been there for years."

"Did they take anything away?"

"No," Ryan answered Liv's question. "I found the bone next to the tree where I dropped it and showed them where I'd found it. They're calling forensics in now."

"What? For a few old horse bones?" Liv screwed her face up.

"There's more to it than that," Ryan said, running his hands through the locks of his bangs again.

"Morgan was poking around on the far side and called Peterson over. There was something half buried, an old boot..."

Ryan looked up at us.

"And they think there might be human bones there too."

Chapter 5

We weren't tired at all that evening when we finally went up to bed. We were supposed to watch a DVD in the nice sitting room, but after the news of what was in the woods we just sat around talking about it. Ryan and I would have to make a statement to the police about how we found the first bone. Morgan and Peterson came into the kitchen for coffee and then returned to the woods to put up some police tape. The warned us that in the morning there would be a lot of people driving through the yard to get up the hill, and even a digger to excavate the pit. The pathologist would be there to study whatever they found and try to find out how long it had been there. Morgan and Peterson were leaving to check missing persons' lists. They figured they could be looking back for a good few years. It was the start of solving a very old mystery.

Whatever had happened in the woods may have happened a very long time ago, but it seemed someone had died – and no one had even noticed. They might not have even been reported missing. What kind of poor person was that? Thinking about the unlucky victim made me feel really sad. Had someone missed the person terribly and never found out what had become of them? Whoever it was had probably been on horseback. What on earth had happened to make them end up dying in a hole in the middle of the woods?

I imagined one of us, going off on our horse and never returning. It made me shiver in horror. And what did the old man have to do with it? Did he know anything? It seemed like he did and he didn't at the same time.

"Morgan was cute," Liv mused.

I'd been waiting for her to say that.

"And about ten years older than you," Rachel pointed out and we laughed.

"Pick on someone your own age," I said.

"Like Hayley did today. She *so* liked Ryan."

"What's new?" I tutted.

"You're right," Liv said. "It was really boring going out with Ry, knowing that everywhere we went girls were going to stare at him. I hated it."

I don't like it, I thought, and he's not even my boyfriend!

That was the problem when you liked the best looking boy in the class. It was pretty likely that a few others did too! There wasn't anyone as nice looking as Ryan at my school. Once, some of my classmates had seen me with him in town. They didn't leave me alone for about three weeks asking questions, and then a couple of them suddenly really wanted to come and see the horses, but Ryan was off on a shoot for a month and their interest trailed off. I'm sure he wouldn't have been too pleased if I had brought three girls around to stare at him.

I told Rachel and Liv about the neighbors the old man had spoken of.

"Where could *they* possibly live?" Liv wondered. "At the power station?"

"I wondered about that," I told her. "He must be stretching the word 'neighbor' because there isn't anyone who lives around here. I mean, where does *he* live? He just appears there. He's like a baddie from one of Tony's video games, there every time you come around a certain corner of a certain level!"

Rachel laughed. "He freaked me out," she said. "Where do you think he comes from?"

She had a really good point. The last time I had seen the old guy was on the way back from showing the detectives the woods. He hadn't been there on the way up the hill and I didn't think it likely that he came from the direction of the clearing or the fields, because I was only in the woods for a few minutes. It would take him longer than that to walk across from the field to where he always was, on the slope overlooking the field. So that meant he had to come from the other side of the river, past the farmhouse. But we'd never seen him coming across the bridge. Plus, there was the fact that the guy didn't seem to be very mobile. I fell asleep thinking it was all too weird.

With breakfast over we headed to the set for our costume fittings. The costume designer's trailer was huge. We knocked on the door and were thrilled to see it opened by Maggie, who had been on a shoot with us earlier in the summer. She was a really lovely lady. Her thick dark red hair was piled on top of her head and she had rimless glasses propped on the end of her nose. She reminded me a little of my mom, early forties and very glamorous. The inside of the trailer was groaning with racks of clothes – mostly old from the musty, vintage smell in the air.

"How's this?" Maggie held up a hanger. I put my hands up to my face and gasped. I wasn't a big fan of dresses – ever, but what Maggie had picked out for me was gorgeous. It was a cornflower blue summer dress in a delicate, flouncy cotton.

"This is a 1940s tea dress. It will look amazing with your hair color."

"Salma, that's so lovely," Liv said. "I wish I was wearing it."

"You just wait, Liv," Maggie said. "Salma, go and try it for size. I'm hoping it will have a little extra room on the waist."

Maggie pointed down the trailer to the curtained off

section. I took the dress into the changing room and slipped it on. It was weird turning to look in the mirror. I never ever looked like that in my life. My mom would have really loved it. She was always bugging me to look girlier. This was beyond girly for me!

I went back to Maggie and the girls.

"You're such a beauty, Salma," Maggie said. "It's perfect."

Liv was grinning broadly, clutching a similar dress in a pretty pink with tiny green flowers on it – and Rachel had a ruby red colored one.

"You're supposed to look like country girls who have made an effort for the show. Like you're wearing your best dresses – 'Sunday Best', as they used to say. I'll have some flowers for your hair too."

"I can't believe we're actually going to be *in* this movie," Rachel said. "We haven't actually been on screen before as ourselves, only as doubles," she told Maggie.

"Will we get an acting credit?" Liv asked.

"Sure." Maggie said.

She turned to the work surface beside her and flipped through what looked like a bound script.

"Fairground horse performers..."

"Is that the script?" Liv asked.

Maggie nodded. "Yes."

The three of us giggled. "Keep it away from me!" Rachel said.

I explained to Maggie while the girls tried on their

dresses. She laughed and decided not to pin my dress. It fell just above the knee and I figured it wouldn't be getting in the way of my gymnastics. I didn't want it to be at all tight, either, which it wasn't. Basically, Maggie had found the perfect one. I also had a pair of matching pants shaped like cycling shorts. I was happy to see them. We weren't doing any upside down stuff like Ryan, but we would definitely need them for the Mills!

Liv pushed the curtain aside dramatically. "Ta dah!!"

The two of them looked great.

"What's Ryan going to wear?" I asked Maggie.

She rummaged on the rack and pulled out a simple outfit of black trousers and a white collarless shirt. "I could put him in a sack and he'd still look good," Maggie laughed, winking at me.

Back at the farmhouse Ryan and Mr. Vazquez were practicing – and they had company. Hayley was leaning against the fence. We heard her long before we saw her – clapping and shouting encouragement. As we came through the gap from the yard she let out an enthusiastic whoop. Mr. Vazquez shot her a look of irritation.

"Look at your dad." Liv nudged Rachel. "She's going to get herself removed if she's not careful."

Hayley turned and smiled at us. "This is *sooo* great!" she said. Ryan came alongside the fence with Red and dismounted.

"Oh! You're not done, are you?" she said.

Ryan smiled. "Almost," he said.

I thought his brightness seemed a little forced.

"Have you been here long?" Liv asked Hayley.

"A couple of hours," Hayley replied. "I need to go back to Maggie now anyhow." She glanced at her watch. "Got another fitting. Will you come with me, Ryan?"

Ryan looked momentarily glazed. "Sure!" he replied.

He passed Red's reins to me and I made a big fuss over the chestnut. Luce whinnied from up at the top of the field with the bays. His form was perfectly outlined on the horizon. We walked around the corner of the field to the grassy path and began ascending the hill as the horses walked over to greet us. We made a huge fuss over them as well and then headed for practice.

An hour and a half later I really thought I was ready – if I were allowed to do it down on the field with no one watching. I just couldn't stop thinking of the two hundred extras and a full film crew. I closed my eyes for a moment and gave a silent prayer that it would all be okay. I was annoyed at my own anxiety. What we were doing tomorrow was what we did in the field at home for fun. I just couldn't get the idea out of my head that we were "The Entertainment." The extras were only pretending to watch, but in my head it was almost worse that they were being paid to watch and cheer. I decided I would much rather we were performing one of our more dangerous stunts with a limited crew for the official show than this easy stuff. I had done okay, though. Better than the day before, and Liv and Rachel said so.

Ryan was away for ages. I tried not to think about it and just have fun with the girls as we did our evening stable chores, but I felt a knot of dread in my stomach about Ryan and Hayley. I consoled myself by being with Luce and the happy thought that I knew he was finally contented here in this strange place after such an alarming start. The horses seemed nicely relaxed after their exercise, and it had been another beautiful, warm, sunny day, with the pleasant hint of a light breeze, so no one had felt too hot.

Just as we were finishing up, the pathologist's van and another vehicle were coming down the grassy path, followed by a police car. They had been up there all day.

As they drove at a snail's pace through the yard, Detective Morgan nodded to us from the passenger seat, through the open window.

"We'll come and talk to you tomorrow," he said. "Interesting day."

We looked at each other, making faces. We were just about to head into the kitchen when Ryan finally appeared. He went over to Red, looking a little distracted. I was at the back door when he called to me.

I went over, unable to ignore Toby who stuck his head out of the next box at the last moment, almost knocking my head off. Toby was the biggest horse I had ever seen. He was immensely powerful but with the sweetest nature you could imagine, if he counted you as one of his friends

– as long as you didn't touch his ears! I played with his super white wavy mane, wondering what Ryan wanted me for.

"Want to go for a walk?" he asked, sounding somewhat nervous. I was reminded of when we had first met, when he had been difficult to talk to, not making much eye contact and generally being aloof. Not that it had kept me from liking him.

I shrugged and gave him a questioning look. "Okay."

Ryan led the way over to the trees and the path. I walked beside him and he started going up the hill. I suddenly felt a strange kind of tension between us. Something was definitely going on.

"I need to ask you something," he said quickly. My heart leapt into my throat. Surely he wasn't going to ask me out, was he? No. It couldn't be that. My heart was hammering in my chest.

"It's about Hayley," he said.

"Oh."

So they were going on a date or something. An hour of clapping and a walk back to the set had done the trick. A good job by her. But I was upset. We kept on walking and reached the plateau. The police tape had been extended to seal off a larger area of the woods. Once again, I found myself up there as it started to get dark and I really didn't want us to stick around for long. I felt a distinct evening chill in the air and pulled my sweatshirt on.

"It's not what you think," Ryan said.

But then we looked up and there, suddenly, was a rider in front of us – a girl, about the same age as us. She had light brown hair in a braid over her shoulder and nice, rather unusual features with good bone structure. Even in the dusk I noticed her sleek, light colored eyes. She rode a large bay dun cob, at least sixteen hands, with a black face and mane. He had a sweet-natured look that won my heart in an instant. They stood there staring at us. I guessed she was one of the neighbors the old man had told me about. Maybe he wasn't so crazy after all.

"Hello," I said, smiling.

She looked at me curiously. Her stocky horse was absolutely still.

"The old man said you might come by."

The girl smiled at me rather vaguely. Ryan was staring at the ground, obviously unwilling to make any attempt at conversation. I was annoyed with him. Whatever he had been about to say to me, there was no need to be rude.

"Do you live nearby?"

"Not far," the girl said. "But I really have to be going now," she added. But she and the horse remained still, like statues.

"You two were the ones who came into the woods, weren't you?"

Ryan looked up then. "Yes. Do you know anything about what happened in there?"

"I really must go," came the reply. "But maybe I'll show you," she added, as she was turning her horse.

"Nice to meet you," I said.

The girl headed off across the clearing toward the field, her thick braid now bobbing up and down against her back. I watched for a moment, and then I realized I was alone. Ryan had already started back to the farmhouse. I jogged after him, turning once to see that the girl and her horse had gone. Where could she be going at this time?

"Another weirdo," Ryan mumbled.

"She wasn't weird! *You* were rude. She probably went off because of your bad attitude."

"If you remember, I was trying to say something important," he said indignantly.

"Okay – what were you trying to say? That you're going on a date with Hayley?"

Why did he feel he needed to break the news to me in this way? Did he think I couldn't take it? The whole thing was getting embarrassing now.

Ryan let out a short laugh.

"No. But she asked me out on a date on the walk back and I said …" he trailed off awkwardly.

"What?"

"I told her I was going out with you."

My head snapped around to look at him. "Why on earth did you say that?"

I didn't mean to sound that incredulous. It just came out that way. Ryan frowned and I saw hurt in his eyes.

"Oh, I'm sorry you think it's such a ridiculous suggestion! Thanks."

71

He strode on ahead and I heard myself laughing.

"Why couldn't you just say 'No'?" I called after him.

I knew why, though. It was the much easier way out, but it was still a big, fat lie.

Ryan turned back to me. He had a face like thunder now.

"It was either you, or I'd have to say Liv, and she drives me crazy!"

"Oh, great!" I flashed. "So it's a complete nightmare – or me. Thanks, Ry!"

Now it was my turn to stride off down the hill. I couldn't believe what I was hearing.

Chapter 6

I felt Ryan's hand on my shoulder. He spun me around.

"It came out wrong just then. I didn't mean it like that," he said.

At least he was looking at me properly now. I stared at his gorgeous face, full of regret as he kept on talking.

"I'm sorry. Look, just forget it. I don't expect you to do anything to help me. I didn't, anyway. But you know what this whole world is like. Could you just … if she asks you … just please try to make me not look like too big of an idiot?"

His brown eyes were so genuine, it was difficult to keep on being annoyed.

"It was stupid of me, I know. I should have asked you first."

He was gesticulating with his hands, thinking hard.

"Don't you like her?" I asked. "She's so pretty – and she's nice."

"Yes, but that's not everything, is it? She's not my type, that's all."

I smiled, secretly glad, but I tried to stay cool and draw the whole discussion to a close without fighting with him again.

"I won't rat you out, don't worry," I said calmly, as I strolled over to Luce, who gave a little whinny as we appeared in the yard.

"Just check with me beforehand next time."

Ryan turned and smiled at me, but he was still looking downcast. I wondered if I should go over to him. Maybe this was the moment I had been waiting for.

"I will," Ryan replied.

He gave a quick glance around the stables and then went in through the back door. I stood with Luce, hugging him and talking quietly into his ear. He seemed to like it when I did that and leaned down toward me.

It had definitely been a strange half hour, starting with the girl up in the clearing. I hoped we'd see her again. Ryan had been pretty rude. I was sure that was why she had gone off so quickly. Or maybe she had been freaked out by the spooky twilight and the woods, the way I was? I still couldn't figure out where she could have been heading off to, though.

Should I have just said, "Okay Ry, that's fine," to the girlfriend thing?

"What should I have done?" I asked my beautiful horse. He pushed against me sweetly.

"Whatever that means," I laughed, and then I gave him a kiss and went in for supper.

"I told you he likes you," Rachel said across the pitch-black room.

We were trying to make it an early night. We'd been told by the makeup and hair girls to wash our hair tonight rather than tomorrow morning since 'dirty hair' was easier to style. With that job done, we settled down to get a good night's sleep, but then I told them about Ryan's proposition. I wasn't sure I should have. For one, I didn't want to annoy Liv, since they used to go out, but I guessed that wasn't really an issue any more. Both of the girls knew that I liked Ryan and there was no point in hiding it. I didn't think I could do that anyway. And now that they were my best friends, sometimes I needed to tell them stuff. Ryan would have killed me, though. He should have been glad I didn't tell them what he said about Liv.

"He does like you," Liv agreed. "And if you're wondering if I'm bothered, I'm really not. He is totally 'Ex.' Really. We are like opposites. I don't even know why we were ever going out in the first place! You and Ryan would be great if you were dating."

"Hmm, I'm not sure," I told them. "He only came out with my name for an easy escape from Hayley. It's not exactly flattering, is it?" I laughed, suddenly remembering

Ryan's room was just across the landing and burying my head under the covers to stifle the noise.

"Salma," Liv started. "I don't mean to sound weird or anything and please don't think I'm trying to pick a fight, but did you ever notice that Ryan and I split up soon after he met you?"

I hadn't thought about that at all. It was true. I felt a glimmer of hope but pushed it away. We had the shoot tomorrow and that was all I could focus on. Two hundred extras, all dressed up and all watching me. I fell asleep with a familiar knot of nerves in my stomach.

Maggie's trailer was an oasis of calm on a totally crazy movie set. I'd never seen a set so busy. All the extras had already been in wardrobe and were over in a huge crowd being briefed by someone on a platform with a megaphone. Rachel, Liv and I had been to makeup and it was time to put on the gorgeous dresses. We stood together in front of Maggie's huge mirror. This time I really didn't recognize myself. My hair was falling in shiny, wavy clumps to my shoulders. With the cornflowers pinned on either side of my head and the striking makeup there was a new me in the mirror. I never wore lipstick, and they had lined my mouth and filled it in with a deep, reddish pink and blotted it and then put another coat on top. The difference was amazing. I didn't think that I looked much like a simple country girl, but I wasn't about to complain.

Rachel looked like a supermodel. Her hair was loose

and they had put in heated curlers, so when it was taken out it was wavy and thick and now pinned back off her face. They had done Liv's hair in a braid with wavy pieces teasing around her face. Liv was obsessed with makeup and wore tons of it, but the girls had done it totally differently to her usual style, with a sweep of black eyeliner over her eyelid giving a sleekness to her wide blue eyes. She looked awesome too.

"You three look amazing," Maggie said, smiling at us like a proud mom. She turned and reached for her digital camera. "Let's take one outside."

We all piled out into the hot sunny day and stood beside the trailer together. Maggie snapped away and showed us the shots. They looked cool. The colors of the dresses together were amazing.

"Thanks!" I said, "My mom will want one of those."

"I'll email it," she promised.

Ryan came around the corner with his white collarless shirt and black trousers. He didn't see us at first, but then he looked up and the coffee cup he was holding twitched to the side, spilling the steaming liquid over the rim. His eyes nearly popped out of his head.

"Wow," he said and we all just laughed. If I was worried that he might be awkward with me after the evening before, that moment took it all away. We all just stood there, looking at each other and giggling, until Mr. Vazquez came over.

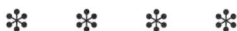

✳   ✳   ✳   ✳

Our part of the first day was more relaxed than I had expected. Mike the Director just told us to do a constant vaulting display, which they were filming from different angles while the crowd milled around and cheered us. We took turns and they shot when we were ready. Mr. Vazquez was in control in the center of the circle, using the lightest touches of his whip and vocal sounds with amazing expertise. All of the horses, including Luce, were used to responding immediately at home – and Rachel and Liv on Chokky and Velvet took all of the practice from our field straight to the set with an effortless transition. I watched, waiting for our turn, as Luce snorted beside me.

My turn in the ring came all too quickly, but the one thing I tried to focus on as we took our starting position was that Mike had said really clearly at the start of the day that he wanted us to look like we were having fun. We were country girls putting on a bit of a circus at the fair. I waited for the signal to "Go" with a smile on my face, patting Luce, determined that I would look as if I was enjoying myself.

It worked! I kept my grin there as we started and half way through I felt like I was smiling for real. Luce knew it too because he was perfect. He responded to the touches of Mr. Vazquez's whip and was more focused than he'd ever been before. But as always, there had to be a little surprise. I dismounted as I finished and there was a burst of applause, which Luce took as a signal to go again – on his own. I realized in horror that he was walking off on a new circle and I followed him, and as he rose to a canter I vaulted up, as the crowd laughed. Mr. Vazquez got the cue and did his job in the center, so I performed a Stand for fun, as more cheers rang out around the ring. We stopped and I slid down on the outside of the circle, smiling and rubbing Luce's nose. Then I took a little bow, laughing for real. I hope the cameras hadn't been rolling, but then I heard …

"Cut!"

I looked over to Mike and the crew and I had finished off right there in front of them. My smile changed to a slightly nervous one as I saw Mr. Vazquez, eyeballing my disobedient horse and then me. Then I noticed the huddle of three important looking men in suits looking over with narrowed eyes, their hands up to their chins, obviously not amused at our extra show.

I looked for Ryan and saw him beckoning us over. As I shot a look back over at the producers' huddle, they were watching me walk away. I had an awful feeling in my stomach.

"Bad boy!" Ryan said to Luce, wagging his finger. But he was grinning. "You did the best thing, once he started off again," he said to me.

"I must have looked like an idiot," I said, downcast.

"No," he replied. "You looked great."

There was nothing to do but to watch Ryan take his turn. I'd made my mistake. Surely no one was going to be too harsh about it, were they? But as I looked over at the men in the suits a third time, they were still watching me and talking all together.

Ryan was amazing, first on Red and then the masterful Toby. Mike told us to join the extras watching the show and the time flew by as Ryan performed his flawless set of vaults over and over again. Red and Toby responded to Mr. Vazquez with perfect obedience, even when the sun beat down with such intensity that it was almost uncomfortable to stand and watch.

When Mike called the final cut to the long shots of our vaulting we all cheered Ryan and ran over to hug him. It was only me who had messed up slightly. I just hoped no one would hold it against me. All the same, I was feeling pretty paranoid about the attention from "the suits." And there was no sign of Hayley.

It was late when we got back to the farmhouse. The horses enjoyed the leisurely ride back home. It was calming for them after such a hot and hectic day with so much going on around them. Now they had us to themselves again. We all seemed a little lost in our recollections of an exhilarating day on the set and I was just so pleased to be riding through the balmy evening air with my horse, knowing that he was happy and that we had done the job to the best of our abilities. Luce had enjoyed it and, apart from that little exuberance, he had been a model of obedience.

All we had to do tomorrow was continue on where

we had left off, and Mike would get the medium shots he needed. We knew we could do it. Tomorrow would be even more fun.

Ryan had been okay, even after he spotted Hayley in the crowd later on. She had a few scenes in the afternoon, but she did have her own trailer and stayed in it between shots, rather than hang out with us, as I am sure she would have done if she hadn't blown it with Ryan. I had been more conscious than usual about where he was. When we weren't riding he was always with me. Nothing changed after we spotted Hayley, only that Ryan maybe looked slightly uncomfortable for a moment.

As we all walked over the bridge the forensic people's minivan was coming out through the yard, followed by Peterson and Morgan's police car. We waited after crossing the bridge to let them pass. Rachel and I were just behind Liv, with Mr. Vazquez and Ryan in front. As the police car passed, the younger, good-looking detective waved out of the window at us and smiled. Liv nearly fell off Chokky as she waved back enthusiastically, leaning sideways so she could easily be seen. Chokky did his best to help her stay up, adjusting to her altered position and trying to balance things, while Rachel and I stifled hysterical giggles behind her.

I watched Ryan as he un-tacked and proceeded with the various end-of-day chores. He had been fine with us all day, even when Hayley was out and about, but I wanted to make sure he wasn't going to be funny with me when we were alone. I was sure he tried to steal a glance at me as I was banking up the shavings. He went inside as soon as we had turned the horses out into the field.

Liv, Rachel and I stood watching Red and Luce gallop up to the top of the field together. Toby stayed by us, always the quiet protector, while the bays stood happily together.

I saw the two riders as soon as they appeared over the brow of the hill. I nudged Liv and nodded toward the horizon.

They were riding side by side and heading down the grassy slope next to the field toward us. My eyes narrowed as I watched them draw nearer – a boy and a girl, maybe the girl from the other evening. Their horses were instantly recognizable as a blue roan and a powerful, jet-black horse, which the boy was riding.

"Really lovely horses," Rachel said. "The black one looks a little like Luce."

She was right. Red and Luce made an enthusiastic pass back down the hill, veering alongside the fence next to the newcomers for a short stretch. They didn't manage to distract the well-behaved horses making their way down the hill. I wondered what they would make of our horses and I was glad I would have the chance to talk to the girl again and maybe find out where she lived.

Except it wasn't the rider from the other evening. I could see that now. The girl smiling across at her

companion had much blonder hair than the girl I had
seen the evening before, and this girl wore hers straight
and loose. Her eyes were different. Nothing like the
bewitching ones I had looked into in the twilight. The boy
had longish brown, floppy bangs. He was tall, with a kind,
open face.

The riders smiled at us as they reached the corner of
the field.

"Hi," the girl said. "You must be the people working on
the movie?"

We nodded.

"Yes, shooting started today," Rachel told them.

"Did it go okay?" the boy asked. "We don't usually
get anything exciting happening around here. When they
asked us to prepare your stables for you we jumped at the
chance. We hope we did a good enough job for you. Did
you have everything you needed?"

Liv nodded eagerly. "Yes thanks, we didn't have much
to do when we arrived."

I hadn't thought about who might have prepared the
yard for us.

"Your horses are gorgeous," I told them. I'd never seen
a blue roan before, and he was stunning.

"Thanks," the girl said. "This is Smoke." She nodded to
the jet-black horse. "That's Shadow."

"We went for the most obvious names," the boy
grinned. "And I'm Ed and this is Fern, my sister."

He really was nice looking, with high cheekbones and

twinkly blue eyes. Fern looked a little younger with the same cheekbones and eyes.

"We've just been for a ride over the fields," she told us. "It's a great place for a gallop."

"We know!" I told them. "We had a great time down there yesterday."

Ed gestured back up the hill. "We were wondering what all that police tape was doing up there at the edge of the woods on the clearing – and we saw the police cars parked up there. Did something happen?"

I told them what Ryan and I had found and what we knew so far. "We're hoping the police will come and tell us what they've discovered."

"Wow, that sounds like something out of a book," Fern said.

"Do you live nearly?" I asked.

"Up at the farm you must have passed on your way in – a few miles that way." The boy pointed over the river and back up the hill. "No one else lives in this valley, except Tom, of course, an old guy. Have you seen him?"

We glanced at each other and nodded.

"He told us about some neighbors we might see – but I thought we met one of them yesterday. A girl with a long braid, riding a big cob. Do you know her?"

The two exchanged a puzzled glance and then the boy shrugged.

"Never seen anyone of that description," he said. "In fact we've never ever come across another rider in the whole time we've been living here."

84

I felt a little involuntary chill sweep down my spine as I frowned back at them.

"Really? She seemed to be from around here. She knew the woods."

Ed looked thoughtful. "We don't come this way often, but we've never seen any other riders before, not in this whole valley. There's nothing that way except the power station, not even a proper beach." Ed pointed over up the hill in the direction of the fields.

"I wonder who the rider you saw could be? We know Tom so it would definitely have been us he was talking to you about."

"She might have been passing through – on a really long trek or something?" Rachel suggested.

I was shaking my head slowly, trying to remember what she had said to me and finding it hard, because it had all happened in the midst of the Ryan situation, and I had been distracted during the whole interlude.

"Not far," that's what she had said when I'd asked where she was from.

"What did you say, Salma?"

I looked up at four quizzical faces and realized I had murmured the words out loud.

"Nothing," I said "Just trying to remember what the girl from yesterday said." I shook my head. "It was too dark for her to be in the middle of a long ride, though she did head off to the fields." I looked up and smiled.

"So there's not even a beach over there?" I wanted to

change the subject because none of it added up. I really needed to talk to Ryan and ask him if he remembered anything else.

"No, there's just cliffs. The nearest beach is a few miles away," Ed told us.

"Maybe we'll have some time before we go to ride out that way with you. Would you like to come in for a drink before you go home?" Liv was addressing pretty much all of this to Edward. He glanced at his watch and made a face.

"Oops! Thanks, but we're a little late."

"Gosh, Ed, we are!" Fern added, flicking her long blonde hair over her shoulder. "We'll try and make it over again before you go, if that's okay?"

"Of course," we all said.

"He's gorgeous," Liv said, nodding at Shadow.

"Thanks," the Ed smiled. "He's a good boy, aren't you?" He gave the sturdy horse a hefty pat on the neck. "Best friend in the world."

I knew exactly what he meant as my horse was suddenly beside me at the fence, nudging cheekily at my shoulder as I stared at Shadow and Smoke. They were a stunning pair.

"Come on," Fern said to her blue horse.

They headed off down the back of the barn to the bridge. The second I saw the last flick of a black tail disappear around the end of the building, Ryan appeared, coming from the yard.

"You missed Fern and Edward," Liv said.

Ryan rolled his eyes.

"Oh that's such a shame," he said sarcastically. "Who on earth are they? More weirdos?"

Liv tutted. "Not at all," she replied.

"They were really nice and very normal," I added. "But it wasn't the girl we met, and they said they've never seen another rider in this valley."

Ryan looked puzzled. "Didn't that girl say she was from around here?"

I nodded. Ryan had been staring at the ground at that point, leaving me to do all the talking, so I was surprised that he remembered anything at all about what the girl had said.

I thought for a moment, trying to picture her up there in the clearing in the half-light. "She said 'not far'."

I shook myself. I was thinking about it too much and starting to give myself a headache. Why did it matter so much?

"She was strange, though," Ryan added. "I thought so, anyway."

I did too. The answer to my own question had come very quickly. That was why it mattered. Something was definitely not right. I could sense it.

"At least the old man isn't as crazy as we thought, though. Those two do know him. His name's Tom," I told Ryan.

"We should have asked them where he lived," Liv said.

"Well, it looks like we'll be seeing them again," Rachel said.

"Hope so," Liv said, raising an eyebrow cheekily in my direction.

We were about to start the DVD when we heard a knock at the farmhouse door. Liv tutted.

"I don't care who that is, I'm watching this movie."

She crossed her arms and rolled her eyes as Mr. Vazquez went to answer the door.

There was a brief exchange of voices before Mr. Vazquez showed Detective Morgan into the sitting room. Liv's demeanor brightened instantly and she moved aside on the sofa so he could sit next to her, flicking the television off with the remote control.

"Thanks, Ramon." He nodded at Mr. Vazquez.

Mr. Vazquez offered Morgan a drink and then went off to the kitchen to get it.

"Good to see you all," he said, nodding politely around the room. "I thought you might like to know what we've discovered in the woods."

We all nodded and sat forward to listen.

"It's okay to tell you, with this being a cold case, theoretically. It appears we may be dealing with a very old missing persons case. It seems likely that you, Ryan and Salma, discovered a horse's remains … and I'm afraid to say that there was a very unfortunate person who died there in that hole too, very likely in the same incident, possibly the horse's rider. Though who that person was or exactly what happened to them, it's too early to say … and we may never know for sure. There was the boot and we also found fragments of a heavy cloth bag of some kind."

Mr. Vazquez came back with a glass of orange juice and handed it to the young detective.

"Thank you." He took a sip and sat back on the sofa. "We're waiting on the results of lots of tests and there are still a lot to be carried out on the remains to try and put a rough date on things. The whole process could take weeks, but now we've excavated the area and removed what we've found. There are a lot of bone fragments to check and catalogue. Then we may have the task of trying to discover who died in there."

"Gosh!" Liv said. "Do you know if it was a man or a woman?"

Morgan nodded. "A female. We're sure of that … Rather disturbing, I realize," Morgan said, looking around at all of our faces.

"How long do you think the bones have been there?" I asked him.

"Hard to say exactly at this stage – and possibly impossible to pinpoint, but the pathologist thinks we are talking in terms of decades, maybe even as long as fifty years. They'll try to narrow it down considerably with technology that wasn't available in those days."

He took another sip of his orange juice. "This valley is quite remote. A lot of the land is owned by the army. The nearest town is fifteen minutes by car. There's only the power station and the small farm a few miles closer to the main road. There is the possibility you could have discovered a shallow grave, but that's looking rather unlikely. We can't say at this stage, but we can't rule it out of course. There are a multitude of sinister possibilities with the known remoteness of this area. Or we could be looking at a tragic accident, especially with the sudden drop in the land level of that hole there."

I was on the edge of my seat, remembering the program I sometimes watched with Tony on the Crime Channel at home. Maybe what Ryan and I had stumbled on would be the start of them solving a very old mystery, just like the stories on the TV.

"I'll need to document your discovery," Morgan nodded at Ryan and me. "Before you go. I hope that's okay," Morgan looked at Mr. Vazquez who was nodding. "It won't be a statement as such, not as detailed. We've never seen anything like this around here. As you can probably imagine, being a detective around here isn't as busy a job as it would be in a big city. We're mostly dealing with crimes involving vacationers."

Mr. Vazquez's cell phone rang and he left the room to answer it.

"Thanks for coming to tell us all this," Liv said.

Morgan nodded at her. "My pleasure," he said and stood up. "Well, I'd better get going."

He smiled and ruffled his sandy hair. He looked more than a little tired. I guessed he had had a couple of long days. He could have gone home early instead of coming

90

back to talk to us. Liv showed him out while we all flopped back down on the sofas trying to take it all in, and then we all started talking at once. The movie would have to wait for another night.

Mr. Vazquez came back into the room, slipping his phone back into his pocket.

"Salma, I need to talk with you."

I followed him into the kitchen, certain I was in trouble for our little extra scene antics. He gestured for me to sit down at the table.

"That was the producer."

I felt my face go hot. Mr. Vazquez took his seat at the head of the table.

"Did Rachel tell you what is this scene we are filming?"

I shook my head. "No." Even if she had told me, I think I still would have answered "No"!

"Is a scene important for one reason," he held up his index finger. "Someone at the fair gives the child an amulet."

I knew what an amulet was. It was like a charm you might wear around your neck on a chain. People believe they can protect you. My mom was interested in things like that.

"The amulet has a symbol on it, and is no important who gives it to her in the story of the film. Is just important that it is passed to her and that she keep it."

I nodded, wondering what all this had to do with me. I remembered again how I'd seen the men in suits watching me, certain it was because of our silly mistake.

91

"The producer want it to be *you* who gives it to the girl, Salma."

I shrank back in my chair, amazement and alarm mixing up in my brain. Mr. Vazquez sighed. "So I told them okay."

I went back into the room and told the others. They were all thrilled. I wondered if Liv might sulk a little over the fact that I'd been chosen. I was doing her a disservice.

"Move over Hayley," Liv said, shooting a cheeky glance at Ryan. He ignored her.

"Are you okay about doing it?" Ryan asked me.

I shrugged. "I suppose so."

I couldn't understand why they had picked me out to be the one to pass the amulet to the child.

"I'll do it if you don't want," Liv said jokingly.

I smiled at her and put my head back on the sofa and stared up at the ceiling. Tomorrow just loomed even larger.

We went upstairs quite early. I wanted to try to get a good night's sleep again. For a strange place, we had all slept soundly every night, even after hearing the devil horse and getting lost in the woods. I had just finished in the bathroom when Ryan whispered my name.

"Come in here for a minute," he said.

His room was as nice as ours, just much smaller, and there was a tiny sofa under the window.

"What do you think about what Morgan told us?" Ryan asked. I sat down on the sofa, stifling a yawn.

"Not very nice to think about, is it? I mean, it doesn't look like the person died of natural causes, does it?"

"Yes, but who could she be?"

"I think the police will find that out eventually."

"Hmm," Ryan looked thoughtful. "Maybe Tom might know something? It depends on if they were here that long ago. Tom has probably been prowling around this valley for about fifty years. He said the woods were cursed. Maybe he does know exactly why?

"We should ask him," Ryan continued. "Anyway, the police will. We should tell them about him. I want to find out more about this place and the old man who lived here. Maybe he lived here for decades too."

"Why?" My eyes narrowed at him. Ryan seemed really fired up about the whole thing.

"I know this sounds weird," he began, a slightly awkward smile creeping across his face, "but I think we found that place for a reason. There are pieces of a jigsaw, don't you think? There's a huge mystery to work out here."

I laughed. "Which is why the police are here. Honestly Ry, you're starting to sound like me!"

"Yes, but the police are starting at the beginning. It's got something to do with this place," he said, jabbing a finger at the floor. "I mean, what is the thunder we hear and the creepy woods – Tom warning us not to go in there. Luce going all Sixth Sense on us. And as if that wasn't enough, there's that girl we met in the clearing. And the screaming horse. I nearly forgot that!"

I hope I wasn't giving him too much of a funny look. It wasn't like Ryan to get all excited like this. I grinned at him. "Why are you so sure?"

"A horse and rider's skeletons were found in those woods, okay? Where are the nearest stables, Salma?"

I looked into his dark eyes, nodding slowly.

"No one lives around here," he went on. "This is the only place."

For the second time that evening I found myself staring up at the ceiling thoughtfully. Ryan had a point. I wished there weren't so many things whirring around in my brain – and then to add to it all, I laid eyes on the loft hatch. It was in the middle of the ceiling above the end of the bed, freshly painted like the rest of the place.

"What?" he said, seeing my expression changing.

"I know where I'd look if I wanted to find out something about the farm."

Ryan looked at me quizzically.

"Where?"

I jabbed my index finger up toward the hatch.

Ryan looked up. He thought for a moment and then looked back at me with a glint in his eye.

Chapter 7

I slept really well again after all. There was something about sinking down into that crisp comforter in the cozy room that made me ready to sleep every night. Despite the lovely hot sunny days we had been enjoying, the farmhouse was very cool at night. For me, there was nothing worse than tossing and turning in a hot stuffy room, so it was great to feel the temperature drop after dark inside the old stone house.

I had no time to worry about my scenes because it was another early breakfast and a ride over to the set by 7:30 a.m. We went straight to makeup and costume. I found out I would be doing my scene before the rest of our riding. It was second on the list of shots so I was glad I would be able to get it out of the way and enjoy the rest of the day. We were all ready again in our beautiful dresses, sorting out some water for the horses, all waiting nervously for my call.

Hayley arrived and went straight to makeup and then costume. We weren't far from Maggie's trailer in our little area, and as Hayley left Maggie to get ready for her first scene, she glanced over toward Ryan. He was sitting next to me. His shoulder was resting against mine. Hayley took this in and smiled at me quickly. I was worried she might turn into a resentful diva and spoil the day for me, but it seemed that wasn't going to happen. It was a little regretful smile she gave me and it made me feel a little sorry for her. She had really, really liked Ryan. As for me acting like I was his girlfriend, I guess it would have looked that way without me doing anything at all. Ryan hadn't really needed to say anything to me that evening. All I had to do to keep him happy was not deny it if she asked me. I wasn't about to do that.

We all watched as Hayley made her way over to the Director's huddle to talk through the first scene. The little girl who I was to pass the amulet to was there too. Mike walked a ten-yard stretch, pointing out where the moving camera was. Every single person in the scene was given a starting point and told what to do and where they should end up. Hayley and the little girl were just walking through the crowd and looking around. The most acting was to be done by the little girl, taking in the bustle of the fair. The camera would mainly be on her, as the main character in the film. The fair was being seen through her eyes.

I watched it all keenly, hoping it might help me prepare for my scene. Then I heard Liv saying a very enthusiastic, "Hello," and Rachel poked me in the shoulder. I turned around to find Fern and Ed had joined us, this time on foot.

"How did you manage to get onto the set?" Liv asked, laughing.

The brother and sister were grinning too and Ed explained.

"Our dad owns this land," he said. "We found out last night that the set was here."

Fern took up the story. "He said he forgot to tell us – or didn't think it would be of interest to us!" she laughed. "We didn't know exactly where the set was except down here somewhere. We don't ride down here often, you see, because the only easy access is from the road and you don't want to be riding on that road when a car is coming down the hill. The passing space is too tight. So we can't see this field from the farmhouse and we don't come from the road much."

"We were having breakfast and chatting about where the shoot could actually be taking place and Dad just said, 'It's down on our bottom field.' I nearly fell off my chair!" Ed told us, pushing his floppy bangs out of his eyes.

Fern laughed. "There we were, thinking we'd do anything to be able to even have a peek at it, and in the end all we had to do was walk up to the security guard and tell him it was our field."

"And say we'd been invited down by some of the crew,

which was kind of a lie, I guess," Ed finished. "But I only said that because it looked like he might not let us past."

"Of course you're invited," Liv said. "You can just hang out with us."

She smiled at Ed and he grinned back in a way that wasn't discouraging. Rachel nudged my arm.

I was glad they had found us. They were good company.

"So what's going on here?" Ed asked, gesturing to the general chaos of the set.

Liv began to explain what the Director was doing.

"That's Hayley Watts," she said. Ed and Fern looked blank, which I was sure would please Liv even more. We all watched as they walked through the scene one last time and the extras bustled past in every direction. It was amazing how it all came together, with everyone simply just walking from A to B and doing what they had individually been told to do. Then just when they were about to do it for real the sun went behind a small cloud and they had to wait. I didn't mind. It gave me a little longer before I would be called over. I tuned back into the friendly chatter as I heard Ryan speak.

"Do you two know who used to live at the farmhouse?"

"An old man – on his own," Fern replied. "He died about three years ago. He was really old though, about ninety, I think. I don't know how he survived down there."

Ryan nodded. "I knew about him – but what about years ago? Who lived there then?" he asked. He was next to me again, propping himself up with his arm across behind me.

Fern shrugged.

"The same old man. The farmer. He's been there, like, forever. Definitely since my dad's had our farm and well before that. Dad grew up here so that would take us back to the 1960s, maybe even further, and my granddad lived here before that."

"Did the old man have any children?" Ryan asked.

Ed looked thoughtful.

"I think he did. I remember my Granddad saying something about that once. That they grew up and left."

He went on. "Something like that, anyway, but I'm talking about fifty years ago, even more. Tom used to live around here then, but he moved away for a long time. We've seen him around and about back here for the last two or three years, I guess, and we got to know him. He told us he used to live here years ago himself. I don't blame the old farmer's kid for wanting to leave this valley. Fern and I aren't going to hang around here after we've finished school, are we Fern?"

Fern shook her head. "Mom took us to the city last year and we loved it. There was so much going on. We're lucky to live here in such a nice part of the country where people come on vacation, but I want something more exciting for my life. I'm not surprised the old man's kid left. Sometimes, down in that valley, it can feel like the end of the earth."

"We hardly ever went down there because the farmer seemed to be a pretty horrible man. He had so many feuds with my dad and Granddad over the years because our land borders his. When we did go for a ride over the river though, in winter, well, it's just not a place you can imagine living."

Ryan was nodding at all we were hearing. He looked at me.

"Interesting," he said, more to me than the others.

I tried to push all the new information to the back of my mind and keep my concentration for events on the set. Then I heard Mr. Vazquez calling my name and felt a bolt of nerves shoot through me.

I walked over to Mike with Mr. Vazquez and shook the Director's hand. He was wearing black jeans, a black T-shirt and a baseball cap with his longish hair poking out around his ears. Directors usually looked disheveled and Mike was definitely in the same club.

In our little huddle were me, Hayley, the little girl named Daisy who was playing the main character Kate as a child, Mike and his assistant Kris. Mike launched right into my instructions.

"Salma, you will be passing the amulet to the young Kate – Daisy here. I want you to dismount from your horse here."

He strode off and turned on a mark and marched back to show my angle of approach.

"You dismount at that starting point and smile and pat

your horse on the nose. You look at Kate and smile and reach into the pocket of your dress."

I fumbled down the side seam and found a pocket that was not there the day before. Maggie must have sewn one in overnight.

"It's a moment between you and the young Kate. It's like you've seen the person who is supposed to have the amulet – like you're a kind of mystery courier and your instructions are to give it to this young girl at the fair. Who you are doesn't matter in the story."

I was nodding to all of this, still amazed that they had picked me to be this odd character – important, but not important. I smiled at the little girl, who seemed so grown up and calm for her age. She was wearing a simple, button-down summer dress. Hayley was wearing a somber green skirt and white blouse with a stylish beige overcoat. What makeup she had was very subtle, but they had made Hayley look like she was in her mid-twenties rather than late teens. It might have been just a hint of shading under the eyes. I couldn't tell, but it was perfect. She was listening carefully to Mike too.

Mr. Vazquez brought Luce over to me, much to the little girl's delight. I looked over to him standing there, his head to one side, staring at us with his soft, almond shaped eyes.

"What's his name?" she asked. I told her, deciding not to tell her his full name, which was Lucifer. Luce nodded and stared calmly at the huddle. I took him over to our starting mark before he did anything silly.

We did one run through of my approach and dismount, which Mike said was okay except I had done the whole thing too fast. Then we got ready to shoot.

"When you're ready, Salma!"

I watched the clapper board snap before the camera as I started my approach. I cantered a few more slides, slowed and slid down from Luce's back, trying to remember everything Mike had told me and to make sure I was on the right mark. I stroked Luce and smiled at Daisy and then went for my pocket, realizing I hadn't been given the amulet yet. I pretended I had it, and after a moment of looking thoughtful I walked over to Daisy, smiled again and held out my hand.

"Okay, good!" Mike shouted.

"I just need the amulet, though," I said tentatively.

Everyone laughed.

"Well bluffed." Mike said. "Dave, we need that prop now!" he shouted.

"Dave" came rushing over and produced the amulet from his pocket. He handed it to me and I turned the object over in my hand. It was a really odd little thing. Something you would expect someone to wear around her neck as a pendant. It was indeed like a charm of some sort, made of flat, silvery metal and it had a symbol engraved on it – a beetle of some kind.

"What is it?" I asked Dave.

"It's called a scarab, a dung beetle, I think," he said. "It's a symbol of resurrection or regeneration, something like that..."

I stared at it some more, feeling suddenly thoughtful. I saw the dead tree in the dark. I saw the pit. I saw the girl on the grassy plateau in the twilight. I saw Detective Morgan speaking of missing persons …

I looked down at the scarab again, thinking about what Dave had told me. Resurrection. And then I felt I knew. The girl with the cat-like eyes that Ryan and I had spoken to up there in the suddenly chilly dusk … maybe she was a ghost.

My hand clasped around the amulet. I slipped it into my pocket and turned for my mark. Suddenly the whole set became the fair. Ryan and the others continued their display as the background to our scene and every single extra was in full flow as a stall holder, a juggler or a fairgoer, chatting and walking along as I did my bit. We went through the shots, with a couple of takes for each one and then the final one of me handing over the amulet to Daisy. Mike did seem very happy with me, shouting, "Very nice, Salma!"

On the last take, Luce followed me over to Daisy and stood next to me as I fished in my pocket. I knew he was there because he was nudging at my side with his muzzle. I patted his neck with my free hand but as I passed the amulet over to Daisy, his head loomed into the shot from the side and everyone fell out laughing.

Mike yelled, "Cut!" and we did it one final time.

Again and again I had stared at the amulet in my palm, before placing it back into my pocket to redo

the scene. It was a mesmerizing little object. I could
have believed it was magical, as it would prove to be
in the story of the movie. But for me it was starting
to symbolize something else; the mystery rider in the
clearing – the girl rider who no one had ever seen before
and who seemed to come from nowhere – but who knew
all about those woods. And now Ryan and I just had to
find out all about her.

Mike was checking the playback on the monitor. They
were all smiling.

"Great work, Salma," he called to me. "We got it all."
And everyone started clapping.

I went over to Luce and hugged him, turning to see my
own crew applauding too. I walked over to them, beaming
a massive smile and feeling like I'd just passed the
toughest school exam with flying colors. It was fantastic,
and now I could just enjoy the rest of the day. Liv and
Rachel gave me a huge hug and then Ryan joined in.

"Well done," he whispered in my ear.

Liv and Rachel broke away and I was left standing
there with Ryan, with his arm around my waist. I glanced
up and, just as I suspected, Hayley was looking over at us.

We raced through the schedule to get all the shots, and it
was relatively early when we crossed the bridge back to
the peaceful surroundings of the farmhouse. I stood with
Luce for a while in the yard before we turned the horses
out into the field and as usual, we watched them settle into

the space. Toby quietly cropped the grass beside the bays and, in contrast, Luce and Red launched themselves at full speed up the hill.

Ryan was beside me. I saw him glance over quickly at Liv and Rachel. They were deep in conversation about the new hot topic, Ed – and they would be for some time. Ryan gestured in the direction of the house.

"Come on," he said.

I frowned at him. "Shall we get them to help?" I asked quietly.

Ryan shook his head. "Dad will wonder where we've all disappeared to; and Liv will probably end up putting her foot through the ceiling. You know what they're like."

I laughed and followed him to the back door.

Half a minute later we were in his room, staring up at the loft hatch.

"Did you hear what Ed said about the old guy having children?" Ryan said.

I nodded. For some reason I wasn't quite ready to tell him about the thoughts that I'd had down on the set when I had held the amulet, but it seemed he was kind of thinking the same thing.

Ryan looked around the room and went for the simple kitchen style chair that was behind the door.

"He said they left, though," I replied, as Ryan put the chair on the bed. I nodded at it.

"That's a disaster waiting to happen. We won't keep it steady."

"Well I don't see a ladder around here, do you? What if the person, let's say it was a daughter… what if she didn't quite leave? We need to find Tom and ask him. I can't believe we forgot to ask them where the old guy lives again."

He put his hands on his hips.

"Right, you get on the chair and I'll hold it steady." I knew better than to argue and stood on the bed. Getting on the chair was much easier said than done. It felt like the first time I tried to stand up on Luce, but eventually I was standing on the chair, on the bed, reaching up to the ceiling.

"I think I can get up there on my own if you can get through the hatch."

The ceiling was just above my head now. I raised my hand to the hatch and pushed. It didn't move. There was no bolt or keyhole. It was just painted down. I gave it a more strenuous shove and we heard a cracking sound as the new paint started to give way. One more push and the hatch moved upwards. I used both hands to lift it up, keep it level and then to push it aside. The day's heat from the loft space reached me immediately. I could see that it wasn't totally dark up there. There was also a hint of light coming through from somewhere.

"There's some light," I told Ryan.

"There's a funny little window you can see from outside," he said. "That's why I wanted to come while it was still light."

I nodded and reached up into the hole, able to lever my elbows up through the square.

"You'll need to lift me up a little," I told Ryan. "I'm not strong enough to do it myself. It needs someone taller."

"Ready?" he called.

"Yes."

Ryan grasped my legs just below the knee and lifted me directly upwards. How he did it while keeping the chair steady I don't know, but a second later I had my hands firmly on either side of the hatch and was pulling myself up into the space. Ryan let go and I heard him swear and looked down to find him spread out, half on the bed and half on the floor. Knowing he would get mad if I laughed I waited for him to join me in the loft, which he did in about five seconds. We waited a moment to make sure no one was about to come in and wonder what on earth we were doing. Nothing. So we looked around the space we were now in. The loft was very large and very empty.

Through the tiny, smudged window I could see Liv and Rachel leaning on the top bar of the fence, still chattering away.

"Looks like it's been cleared out," Ryan said. "It's worth a look around, though. The ceilings in the bedrooms aren't new, so they didn't gut the place. This would have been the original loft floor, so there might be something."

I doubted it.

Ryan went off across the length of the space in the

direction of the other tiny window on the far side, which I guessed must face the river. He was balancing on the beams and using the struts of the roof to keep himself steady. If he slipped we would go crashing through into a bedroom below – and knowing our luck it would be Mr. Vazquez's room while he was having a late *siesta*. I imagined the scene for a moment and then wiped it from my mind. It did not bear thinking about! We'd come a long way since the bickering and trouble when we arrived and I prayed nothing would happen to land us back in it now.

"Just be careful," I whispered as loudly as I dared. Ryan turned and nearly slipped, grabbing for a lintel above his head.

"I will if you don't say anything to me!" he said.

I decided to poke around in the area near the hatch where there were at least some floorboards. It was obvious that the loft had been cleared recently as I could see dusty outlines on the boards where objects had once stood. There were areas with the outlines of packing cases and what looked like the outline of a large trunk – a rectangle with rounded edges. I looked up at the roof and it looked newly insulated. There was no way anything could be left around here that would give us any clues. Ryan was coming back toward me.

"Nothing," he said. "There's enough light to see all around there, even in between the beams."

"What are we looking for anyway?" I asked him. "We're hardly going to find a diary, are we?"

I looked over toward the grubby window on my

side of the space. Suddenly I saw the tiniest fraction of something sticking up between the floorboards, just below the glass pane.

"Maybe just an old letter or note," Ryan added, "something that might give us some ideas about anything that happened down here or who lived here. Some newsprint … I don't know," Ryan said.

I went over to the window carefully. The boards had been roughly placed, the weight of the objects and gravity all that was keeping them in place. What my hawk-eye had spotted was a piece of card – just a corner, poking up, as if it had actually been on the floorboards but had fallen off the end into the hole between the lintels that formed the floor of the loft. Or it could have been hidden there. It had turned a mustard-yellow with age. I reached for it, but it felt heavy and the reason for this was because it was attached to a bundle of things tied up with a piece of string. I could see the tiny package clearly now, and lifted it out of the hole. I looked at Ryan as I held the discovery in my hand. His eyes widened and he stepped carefully toward me. The boards moved as he took his last step and he nearly lost his balance. My hand flew out to him and he grabbed it to steady himself and then stand next to me. He stared at my discovery, but he did not let go of my hand. When I looked at him, his gorgeous brown eyes were looking into mine.

"Hayley's not here now," I whispered. I was more nervous than I had ever been in my whole life. I just kept on looking into those eyes.

"I know," he replied and then he smiled. "Salma, I …"

Then we heard Mr. Vazquez calling us from down below in the house.

Ryan muttered grumpily and we both made for the hatch.

"We'll be all right," Ryan whispered. "He's called and we haven't answered, so he'll go down to the yard."

"But he'll see I'm not there either and come back into the house to look for both of us. Come on. Quick!" I hissed.

Ryan jumped down through the opening first and landed on the bed. The chair had fallen off when he had a mishap on the way up. I dangled my legs through the hole and decided to let myself drop down too, clutching the bundle of old paper. Ryan kind of caught me, slung the package under the bed then flew over to the chair and placed it back behind the door.

"Wash your hands!" he said. I heard the back door shut and Mr. Vazquez calling again, sounding impatient now.

"Ryan!"

He said something in Spanish and started coming up the stairs as we dried our hands. We both sat down on the sofa as he opened the door. We looked odd and we hadn't gotten our story straight.

"Where you been?" Mr. Vazquez demanded irritably, "having me hunt the place for you."

"Sorry. We were in Salma's room listening to her MP3 player." Ryan smiled.

Genius. I thought.

"Sorry. We didn't hear you calling." I added.

Mr. Vazquez's eyes narrowed at us both. He just stared at us like he did when he knew we were lying. We did the same thing as usual and looked back at him, trying to appear earnest and convincing. Never break eye contact. That was the first rule!

"Then how you know I was calling?" he said.

I didn't think he wanted an answer. He knew we were fibbing, but he didn't know why.

He looked at us both, but he didn't look that annoyed any more and turned for the door.

"Ryan. You help me in the kitchen tonight starting in five minutes."

"Will do," Ryan called.

He stood and I saw the horror on his face as he realized at the same moment as I did that we had not replaced the loft hatch. Checking to make sure Mr. Vazquez had gone to the kitchen, we used the chair and replaced everything as we had found it.

I checked the bundle which was safely hidden under the bed and told Ryan I was going to my room.

"We'll look at it later," he said.

I nodded as he turned and went downstairs. I lay on my bed trying to calm down for a moment. I resisted the temptation to go back to Ryan's room and retrieve the mystery bundle. It would probably be nothing of interest. Why would we go up there and find exactly what we were looking for? That only happens in stories. But then why did I have the feeling that what was in that bundle was indeed exactly what we wanted?

Liv and Rachel were still talking out by the field. Half of me wanted to go and join them, to get the latest on Ed no doubt, but the other half of me felt like falling asleep in the peaceful room – and that's what I must have done, because the next thing I knew I was being called down for supper.

It was funny watching Ryan's fake yawns and expressions of tiredness as we sat in the living room watching TV that evening. Mr. Vazquez had been giving us both funny looks all evening. I avoided eye contact with him over dinner but then he seemed to want to make fun of us because when I went to see Luce after the meal he called "Ryan will follow shortly" after me. Liv and Rachel looked confused but I wasn't about to tell them what we were up to, or about what had happened in the loft between us. In any case, it was not quite what Mr. Vazquez thought it was.

Out in the yard we agreed to look at the bundle after we'd all gone upstairs. Liv and Rachel were in full gossip mode in the living room in front of the TV and Mr. Vazquez had unexpectedly said he was going out for a while with some of the crew. He'd left at 9 o'clock, saying he would be back after a couple of hours, so it was easy to go and be with Ryan. He seemed to want to keep the girls out of it for now – and I was, of course, happy to be on my own with him!

Back in the cozy little room Ryan reached under the bed and brought the bundle out for us to have a good look at. It did seem to consist of a pile of cards – postcard size. They were very old and dusty, and curled at the edges slightly. The string was a dark colored waxy twine that Ryan was determined not to cut. He struggled with it and then passed it to me for my nails to work on. I unpicked the knot in no time.

"I did all the hard work, obviously," Ryan said. I aimed a swipe at his shoulder with the little package in my hand, sending a cloud of powdery dust into the air which we immediately started to choke on.

"Careful!"

I was laughing. Ryan rolled his eyes and laughed too. "You fool," he added quietly.

I carefully undid the loose knot that was keeping the bundle together and laid the two ends apart. I knelt back on the floor and nodded at Ryan.

"You take a look," I told him.

We stared down at whatever was on the top of the bundle. Whatever it was had been placed face down. Ryan picked it up carefully and turned it over. It was an old black and white photo of the farmhouse with no date on it. Ryan placed it aside wordlessly and we went on to the next thing on the pile, which we could see was another photo, face up, of the farmhouse. Underneath was another, of the yard this time, empty but clearly in use, with a rake placed next to one of the open half doors. I could make out a full hay net hanging inside the stable. Next was the yard again with two horses tethered to the rings beside their stables, under the overhanging roof. The picture was taken from the side. Ryan peered more closely at the horses before turning the photo over to check once again for a date. This time there was one. 1962 was written in blue fountain pen ink.

Ryan said the date out loud and turned the photo over again to the picture side.

"Nice pair of horses," he said, again peering very closely. He frowned and looked as if he was going to say something but didn't. We laid the photo aside with the others we'd already seen.

Next was the same photo from further back, the same horses – and then again in the field, standing together. Ryan picked the photo up to reveal the one beneath it, the last photo. We both gasped and looked at each other. I swallowed.

"Can't be!" Ryan said, drawing in a breath. But it was.

The last photo showed just the one horse in the field, this time with a rider. We had seen the rider before; we had met her and spoken to her. It was the girl from up in the clearing in the twilight. It was definitely she. She had her hair in the same braid, and now I knew that this was the same sweet horse too. Unlike the other evening, though, the expression on her face was very happy. Here, her amazing eyes dazzled, and her smile was full of delight. It looked as though it was for the person behind the camera. I wondered instantly who had taken the picture.

"Check the date," I said breathlessly.

The photo looked as if it was from the same set as the others. Black and white printed on the same paper. Ryan turned it over slowly. There it was. 1962.

Chapter 8

Ryan and I looked at each other. So this was the girl from the farm. The same girl we had spoken to at dusk up by the woods. She was our ghost. What else could she be, up there talking to us face to face on the same horse nearly fifty years later? But was it her bones they had found in the woods? I brushed the thought of it from my mind as Ryan spoke.

"It's her," he said. He stood and started pacing the room. "I can't believe it … but it is her from the other evening. Definitely. I have officially seen a ghost! No. There must be another explanation," Ryan was shaking his head and staring at the wall. "I don't want to think I've gone crazy."

"You haven't gone crazy, Ry. We've seen ghosts before. Lots of people see ghosts."

"Yeah, but …" Ryan's words were cut off by the sound of the screaming horse echoing around the house once again. It was exactly the same sound as it had been the first time. It was another part of the puzzle.

"Come on," Ryan said, scrambling to his feet and making for the door.

Liv and Rachel had rushed up the stairs.

"You hear that too?" Liv's eyes were wide.

"Yep" I replied and started down the stairs after Ryan. "You two coming?"

They both shouted after me at the same time.

"No way!!"

I laughed as I went out into the dark. As I pulled the door shut behind me the stillness of the night suddenly felt immense next to the silent river. I saw Ryan disappear around the corner into the yard. He had stopped running. We knew better than to tear up to the stable and create havoc.

He threw a bridle to me and Luce was thrilled when I slotted the bolt back. He was a big fan of surprise night rides with me. When my family had first moved in across the field from the stables, I used to go and visit Luce down in the field when he came over to our side. He was troubled and no one could get near him, but we soon formed an unbreakable bond. One of the things I used to do was ride him, bareback in the dark. I'd felt a compulsion to do it and he used to wait for me, below my window. Our secret night rides ended when Ryan discovered me one evening. Suddenly he was there in the field, demanding to know what I was doing. I'd watched him from across the field and wondered about him, about the five amazing horses they kept – and then there he was shouting at me in the dark. Our friendship started there, on shaky ground.

Now I turned Luce in a half circle and vaulted onto his back. Every fiber of him rippled with anticipation. Ryan made sure the others were okay and was ready with Red.

"Up to the clearing," he said and started out of the yard.

"Okay," I shouted.

And then we were out of the yard like something out of one of our movies. We cantered up the hill through the suddenly chilly evening air. I loved every second of it. But as we crested the hill to the clearing, well away from the lights of the farmhouse, I realized that we were once again tearing around in the dark on horseback in more than spooky surroundings – and this time we really didn't know what we were doing. We'd heard the terrifying scream of the stray horse and now we were trying to find it. A big part of me knew that it was no stray horse. The sound of him was just another part of the jigsaw. So was the thunder that rumbled again now in the distance, part of the phantom storm that never revealed itself.

Ryan and I halted at the center of the clearing.

"What now?" I said breathlessly.

Then I shuddered as a deafening rumble of thunder erupted over our heads. I hadn't seen any lightning. I looked up and the first thing I saw was the moon shining

brightly over the fields against the inky blue night sky –
and then the stars – hundreds of them. It was a clear night.
There were no clouds on the horizon. So why this thunder?
It was all too weird.

"Where's that storm coming from?" Ryan said warily.
"It's like the other night."

The thunder rumbled again. Every muscle of my
horse's body was tense and Red had a totally manic look
in his eyes.

"I don't like this," I said, as Luce began to prance
and whirl. But then he made a dart forward to the trees. I
reminded him I was on board but I let him move forwards.
We headed for the woods. Again.

"Don't let him, Salma!" Ryan called. I stared ahead at
the trees around the edge of the open space. Luce moved
at a tense but determined trot. I realized with some relief
that we weren't heading for the same point where he had
found the dead tree, the pit and the bones. He was taking me
further to the right – and I wanted to know where. Ryan and
Red followed. I knew he wouldn't let me go alone.

The broad trunks of the chestnut and sycamore trees
loomed in front of me again. Luce stopped for a second.
I thought I heard something in the woods, like a twig
snapping. Luce's ears flicked as he stared into the trees,
and then he took me in there.

"We need a flashlight," Ryan said.

"Too late for that," I called back. Luce picked his way
forwards. I almost wanted to close my eyes, but I knew

that he knew where he was going and that another part of the mystery was about to fall into place. I trusted him totally at that moment, just as he trusted me when he needed my reassurance.

We were now ten yards in, then fifteen. I was suddenly aware of the pale moonlight helping us to see our way despite the heavy tree canopy. I looked ahead, amazed at what was now revealed.

"It's a path, Ry!"

Ryan and Red came alongside as Luce gave a little whinny. The trail was narrow but it was definitely there, heading on into the woods. I patted Luce's neck. He felt calm, but I wasn't and I doubted Ryan was either.

"Daylight is looking like the appealing option," Ryan whispered dryly. "Why did he have to find it *now*?"

I wanted to laugh but concentrated on thinking about what to do next, hoping we wouldn't hear the horse's scream again. Luce certainly knew how to keep us on the edge of our seats – or scare our pants off, more like!

"Your dad won't be back for ages," I whispered.

"So what!" he replied quickly. "Are you enjoying this?"

I realized with a jolt of surprise that I actually was.

"Maybe there's something to find right now," I told him. "Are you scared?"

I hadn't meant it as a challenge. Ryan's frown was suddenly illuminated as a flicker of sheet lightning strobed through the trees.

"Now we really are in the wrong place. Let's go!"

I put my hand up. The lightning had clearly shown the path ahead. I was, I realized, as scared as Ryan, but the same message was playing on in my head. "We're here for a reason."

Luce walked on.

"Salma!!" Ryan hissed behind me as we heard a new rumble of thunder.

We advance about five yards before Luce stopped again. I looked up and saw the moon.

"Salma, we need to get out of this storm."

"There is no storm. Look at the sky." I couldn't quite believe what I was saying.

"Explain the thunder and the lightning then, you idiot!"

"Just a minute," I hissed back. "Then we'll get out."

I stared ahead at the trail. The lightning flickered again, illuminating everything with its stark white light. It was like lightning I'd seen at a school play. It was somehow not quite real. It was, I was certain, another part of the jigsaw. It came again and this time I saw something.

A short way along was a figure, standing to the side of the path.

Luce reared and my heart leaped into my mouth. Ryan swore. But I recognized the figure. It didn't make me any less terrified at that moment – but I had seen him standing there like that before when he had been watching us in the field from under the first line of trees. It was Tom, the old man.

I dismounted and walked forwards, seeing clearly now

that he was standing there at the edge of the path in a shaft of moonlight.

I called his name softly.

"Tom."

He remained still, doing nothing to indicate that he had heard me.

"Tom," I called louder.

I saw him shudder, suddenly aware that he was not alone. He did not turn to me and now I was within touching distance of him.

"You heard that poor animal," he said. It took me a second to remember the scream of the horse, since so much had happened in between. I nodded at the old man.

"Yes, we did,"

Ryan approached, leading Red and Luce on either side of him.

"My horse knew you were here," I said.

Tom nodded slowly. "Aye," he said calmly. "I told you your boy knows things."

He suddenly turned to me, making me jump. "Didn't I?"

"Yes," I replied quickly.

"Where is the loose horse?" Ryan asked softly. "Did something happen here?"

Tom turned away and started across the path again. He nodded, closing his eyes and squinting them shut. Then he shook his head.

"That poor girl," he said. "Her life was bad enough

without dying like that. In that way. It should have been the father that was took." I saw a tear glisten on his cheek.

"Fifty years, and not a day goes by where I don't think about them – and now I know. I spoke to the police. I know what they found. They found my girl, that's who they found."

I saw the photo of the happy rider flash across my mind and looked at poor old Tom, crying in the woods. I knew that he was the keeper of a big part of the mystery.

"We need to take you home," Ryan said, supporting the old man and putting an arm around his shoulder in a way that made me feel like crying myself. I took the reins of our two horses. They seemed calm, considering what had happened.

"She was my sweetheart," Tom cried. I swallowed hard.

"Where do you live?" Ryan asked him. "We'll take you home. Is it far? It doesn't matter how far it is, we'll get you home."

"Far?" Tom said. "It's just this way,"

Ryan turned and shot me a puzzled look. Surely no one really did live in the middle of the woods?

We followed the path, and after a short way it branched off to the right. Tom pointed in that direction and we began heading down the hill through the trees. It was the same hill as the field behind the farmhouse.

I led the horses, following Ryan and Tom as they made slow progress ahead of me. Ryan was patting Tom's shoulder, like a father consoling a son who'd just lost a school football game. We passed another path leading off to the right. I still knew where we were. It was a good feeling in these, the scariest of woods. I thought of the path we had just passed, and a little light switched on in my head. Now I knew how Tom always just appeared at the edge of the trees to watch us in the field. He came this way, through the woods. No wonder we'd never seen him walk past the farmhouse or up from the fields and across the clearing. But what else did the trees conceal? Did he have a hut somewhere? I followed them down the hill and finally saw where we were heading. It was obvious now, though none of us had ever guessed it for a moment. We'd just assumed the little workers' cottages that faced the river on the other side of the stables were empty and derelict. But now we headed down toward the back of one of them and I saw a little yellow light on inside.

Ryan pushed the back door open. I tethered Luce and Red to a downspout just outside and followed him and Tom into the old man's home.

Ramshackle was pretty much how you would describe what we found. There was an ancient gas stove and nothing that looked newer than fifty years old: a simple wooden table with two mismatched chairs, beige walls, and an iron kettle that wouldn't have looked out of place in a museum. There was a saucepan and two plates placed neatly on the side. It was tidy, but there was an old, musty smell. It broke my heart that Tom lived all alone like this.

Ryan helped him into one of the chairs. Tom pointed

ahead to the shelves in the alcove. On one of them was a bottle, with a glass set beside it.

"I need a measure of that, Ryan son," he said calmly.

Ryan took the bottle of medicine and unscrewed the cap.

"Two fingers worth," Tom instructed, as Ryan began to pour. Ryan looked confused for a moment then poured out the liquid using his first two fingers as a measure at the base of the glass. He set it down in front of Tom and sat in the other chair. I stayed standing by the stove.

"Can you tell us what happened all those years ago, Tom?" Ryan asked gently.

Tom closed his eyes and nodded. He took his medicine and looked at Ryan. "I can now, lad," he said. "I thought she had gotten away from the old tyrant. I knew she was going. It was all planned. I helped her plan it."

"Was she the girl who lived in the farmhouse? The farmer's daughter?"

Tom nodded.

"My girl," he said, and his voice began to shake. "Her name was Sally."

Tom let out a sob, the sound of her name clearly so painful to him.

"Was she running away?" Ryan asked.

Tom held is face in his hands and rubbed his cheeks rhythmically. He stared across the room, as if he was replaying the past and seeing it all again. Then he looked up at Ryan and me.

"That man made her life a living hell. I'd only been

here six months working for him but it was enough to
know what she had to put up with." Tom told us. "She
wanted a better life for herself, a life without being
shouted at and beaten and kept a prisoner down here. The
mother, she was kind enough, but there was nothing she
could do to make anything better. The first son, he died
an infant, you see." He looked up at us. "And then Sally
was born and she was meant to be a boy. She could never
do anything right, from that first day. I heard him beating
her... We had to talk in secret. He would have killed her
if he'd known about us. I'd fallen in love with her, see.
She had these beautiful eyes, the lovely hair, but she was
a sweet person. Determined, but so, so sweet, and kind
despite what she had to put up with."

Tom stared down at the table, shaking his head slowly.

"Then one day he found us on the path down by the
river and dragged her away, beat her and locked her up for
a week. The mother gave her food even though she was told
not to. I saw her one more time after that, when she told me
she was going to run away. We decided to go together."

Tom smiled momentarily at this moment of optimism in
the story.

"Her mother agreed to get her out, even though she
knew she would never see her daughter again. But it was
the only way, you see. We just prayed the farmer never
found out that she had helped us."

Tom paused and took a deep breath, no doubt preparing
himself, and us, for the final tragic part of the tale.

126

"But something went wrong, didn't it?" I said gently. Tom lifted his gaze to me.

"It did," he answered. "We were supposed to slip away on Saturday night. I waited for that day. The minutes seemed like hours and the days like weeks. On the Friday there was a great storm. Never heard anything like it. I couldn't sleep. I knew something was wrong. But no one would ever have gone out in that. I heard the lightning strike the woods … And now I think, well I just know that it took my Sally."

I stared at Tom and pushed a tear away from my cheek.

"They were just really unlucky," Ryan said.

Tom took a deep breath. He fumbled in his pocket and wiped his eyes with a checked handkerchief.

"The storm that night was the biggest storm in living memory. There's never been one like it since. It was so hot that day you could hardly breathe, and then those black clouds came in. I'd never seen anything like them. I went indoors and waited for it to come. But …"

Tom waited while the next words danced on his lips.

"I thought I heard Sally's horse, but with the wind and all the other monstrous noises from the storm, I couldn't be sure …"

Tom shook his head.

"I should have gone out there … but I didn't. I found out the next day she had gone that night – one day early. She took her horse and rode off through that storm and away, while her father was out securing the bottom barn.

Her mother told me. She couldn't wait that one extra day for me. That's what I thought. But I was just so glad she got away. She had to get away."

"But did anyone go and see what had happened in the woods?" Ryan asked.

"Why would they? Sal had got away. The old man never went into the woods up there. He was scared of them. He used to say they were cursed before that night … it looks like he was right. I just prayed she was safe."

"But didn't you wonder why she didn't get in touch ever?" Tom sighed.

"It wasn't like it is now, you know, with cell phones and all that nonsense. It would have been a risk for her to try. I spent days up in the town thinking she'd somehow find me or might have left word. I had to be careful who I asked in case they reported back to him, see? In the end … well, I just decided she'd gotten away and … she'd had to let me go too – to leave the past behind. God had decided that we should not have gone away together and I had to live with that. The farmer found me the next day and gave me half an hour to leave this valley with my life. The old man knew she'd run away. Do you know what he said to me? 'Good riddance!'. I spent those weeks after in the town, but when I got no word of Sal, I went away from here for more than forty years. I tried to forget all about her. But I knew I had to come back one day. I had a wife, but she died too. After she passed away, I'd tried to find traces of Sal. There was nothing, so I came back here, to the town. When I heard the farmer had died I moved in here. I had the best times here with Sal, even though it was short. But I couldn't bring myself to go in the woods up there. I felt something … when I got close. I started to think the farmer was right about them being cursed. I've no idea why he thought that, mind you. Probably just another way of controlling people."

Tom looked at me. "Anyway, that was why I told you girls not to go in there. I didn't know what I meant at the time. I just had a really bad feeling."

He took a deep breath. "No one knows I'm here. You won't tell, will you? It made me happy to be back here. I swore I'd find her and I felt her close here."

"We have found her, Tom," I said gently. Tom stared into his glass.

"Aye," he said. "I think we have."

He looked up at us, nodding with the hint of a smile. "I thought I saw her riding the other day, in the twilight. I sensed her near me," Tom said. "Losing my mind with it all now."

"You're not losing your mind, Tom." Ryan said quickly. Tom turned to him.

"Sally … we've seen her too."

Chapter 9

We left Tom there after we'd told him everything about
our stay, from Luce acting up, to us seeing the ghosts
in the clearing, going into the loft and finding the photo
and working out who Sally was, to how we had come to
find him in the woods that night. Tom smiled when I told
him about the photos. He told us that he had borrowed
a camera and taken them when the farmer was away. So
that explained Sally's smile. He said he'd given them to
Sally and she had hidden them in the house so her father
wouldn't find them. She'd hidden them pretty well. I felt
odd thinking that the last person to touch them before me
had probably been her.

We didn't want to think about the night of the storm
and what had happened to Sally. Why had she been in the
woods anyway?

There was another thing he told us that I couldn't make sense of. In ten years since he'd been back at the farm and roaming the paths in the woods, he had never seen the ghosts of Sally or heard the thunder – or the phantom horse. The first time that had happened was on the night we arrived. It was like it was because we were there. It was like we were somehow part of the mystery. But how could that be?

We led Luce and Red around the side of the house and back along the river to the yard. All that time, Tom had been just a few yards from us.

It felt like we'd been out for hours, but it was only about an hour and a half. We had plenty of time to settle the two horses back into their boxes and say a long good-night to all the horses. Luce was calm and happy, pushing at me as Ryan and I talked over the evening's escapades and revelations.

"Poor Tom," Ryan said. "Haunted by memories for most of his life."

I'd been thinking the same. I felt bad that we'd been freaked out by him. He was so harmless – and troubled and sad, roaming around the place trying to feel close to a girl from fifty years ago. And now it seemed that what actually happened had been more awful than anyone could possibly have imagined.

"It's like we're somehow part of it, though," I offered. I expected Ryan to laugh at me, but he didn't.

"Maybe it's not over," he said.

Then Liv and Rachel were at the back door.

"Where *have* you two been? We've been worried sick!" Liv blurted.

"We started up the hill but got scared and ran back." Rachel told us.

I smiled at them

"Lots to tell you," I said, and then the distant sound of a car heading down into the valley sent us all scurrying into the house.

I lay in bed with the images of Sally's smiling face imprinted on my brain. Maybe now that we thought we knew how she had met her end, she could find some peace – and so could Tom.

Our final day on the set was great. Mike was just after a few final shots and we were back in the lovely dresses for the last time. The only problem was that it was just a little too hot and humid.

Hayley was around us a lot and we chatted and had fun, even if she was a little sheepish around Ryan, and he the same with her. At lunch I went over to the catering tent and suddenly Hayley was beside me in the line. She put her hand on my arm.

"I'm sorry, I didn't realize Ryan was your boyfriend. I don't want you to be angry with me."

I looked at her, remembering the boyfriend thing. I didn't know what to say. She really seemed to care what I thought of her.

"It's okay," I replied. "You didn't know."

"But I should have," she insisted. "He's obviously crazy about you. I'm really sorry."

I sighed inwardly. "No, it's really fine." I spied Ryan looking over at the two of us – a mixture of curiosity and anxiety on his face.

"No, I should have known." She looked suddenly very sad. "Sorry," she said, brushing away a tear and taking a deep breath. "It's hard trying to find a nice guy in this job, you know," she laughed.

I hugged her.

"It's hard to even find a friend, and the next thing you know things are being made up about you. It was nice to hang out with you guys today. I wish we had another day together."

She had pulled herself together. I was glad. I didn't think I could deal with the idea of another sad life. I thought of all the amazing actors she would get to meet that we could only dream of standing in the same room as!

I smiled at her. "Just try and have fun and someone will come along when you least expect it," I said, remembering something I'd heard my mom say on the phone to one of her friends.

Hayley nodded. "I guess you're right," she said.

"No being sad," I said jokingly. "Maybe we'll work together again."

"Can we keep in touch, Salma?" Hayley asked. "It's so nice to talk to you. Who knows," she grinned, "you were so great in front of the camera we might actually act together one day!"

I laughed at that. As if!

Hayley got out her smart phone and I gave her my email.

"Cool," she said. "Thanks."

We hugged again and she went off happy.

The rest of the day went so quickly. Ryan was really showboating toward the end. He was just fabulous at everything, and my heart was bursting with pride as the extras clapped and cheered his wonderful vaulting. There was a huge cheer when Mike shouted.

"THAT, ladies and gentlemen – is a WRAP!"

Everyone started to drift away. I went back to Luce and the others, looking forward to being back at the farmhouse and finding some cooler air.

"This is the hottest day so far," Rachel said, fanning her face with a piece of card.

"There's a massive storm forecast for later." Maggie said a few minutes later, as I passed the dress back to her on its hanger.

It was the last thing I wanted to hear. I changed the subject.

"Bye, dress!" I said. "It was nice knowing you!"

"Can I keep mine?" Liv asked in the style of a six year old.

Maggie laughed.

"I'd love for you to keep them because you all wore them so well, but yours, Liv, cost me two hundred dollars on an auction website."

Liv smiled and shrugged. "It was worth a try, I guess."

We all hugged Maggie goodbye like a favorite aunt.

"See you on the next picture," she said. "Oh, and I'll send you that photo. Tell Ryan he'd better come and say goodbye too,"

Ryan appeared at the trailer. "As if I wouldn't," he said, turning on the charm.

Mr. Vazquez was shaking hands with Mike and the producers and we all did the same as the set was dismantled around us. I stood with Luce as the gypsy wagons were towed away and the straw bales were loaded up onto Fern and Ed's dad's trailer.

Ryan returned, grimacing at the heat.

"It's not funny any more," he said. "I'm wilting here."

"They're not liking it either," I said of the horses. Luce had been snorting and seemed unsettled. Being non-fading black, he always struggled with extreme heat.

"He can probably sense the massive storm everyone says is coming," I said.

Ryan looked dismissive. "Not for a while yet," he said. "We'll have time for that ride with Fern and Ed."

"We'd better have time," I said. "Or Liv's going to lose it completely!"

I looked up at the sky. It was a slightly hazy blue. The

air around us was so muggy that we could almost feel the pressure building up.

The horses were all glad to be on the move and to feel some air moving around them. We were happy to reach the yard and the shade of the old stone house. The horse boxes with their stone walls at the back felt cool, so the horses had some relief. Apart from that, we just had to wait for the sun to go down and the rain to come.

When Fern and Ed arrived for the ride there was no sign of any black clouds on the horizon. We left Mr. Vazquez checking the tack and preparing the transporter for the long journey home.

"I no want you in my way 'ere anyway," he said. "Go enjoy your ride." And he waved us away cheerily with the back of his hand. He was in a great mood now that the shoot was over and we'd done a great job. It was mission accomplished again. It was all that mattered to him: that, his children and his horses.

Fern and Ed were as cheerful as ever. I loved them. They were just so friendly, nice and funny.

Ed looked up at the sky as the six of us rode up the hill.

"No sign of that storm," he said. "Probably won't materialize. They're always wrong these days."

"We'll just keep an eye out," Ryan said.

"Yep, sure," Ed agreed. "The last place you want to be stuck in bad weather is out on the fields."

Liv fell in next to Ed at the front followed by Fern and

Rachel, with Ryan and me at the rear. Luce felt a little prickly but I guessed I would be too if I were wearing a black coat in ninety-five degrees all day. It wasn't going to be a long ride, but it would be proper exercise for them.

Ed and Liv seemed to be getting along really well. I was happy for her and smirked to myself as I heard her best flirtatious laugh ringing out from under the passing trees. Liv spent most of her time liking boys she had no hope of going out with – like the nice police detective. But then again, this being our last day and us being from a different part of the country, it wasn't like Ed was about to become her boyfriend either. I looked across at my fake boyfriend Ryan. Or was he so fake? That moment in the loft. What was he about to say to me? I was so overwhelmed by it all I had almost blotted it out. Had we missed our chance?

We reached the clearing and my eyes were instantly drawn to those woods. Ryan and I halted, our thoughts surely the same. The others went ahead to the top of the slope. I suddenly felt an immense chill in the air that was beyond strange. I looked at Ryan.

"First sign of the storm, probably," he said. "We'll have to watch out."

I remembered the last time I'd felt a sudden chill. And the time before that. In the dark, when something was about to happen. When there were ghosts. It was only now that I'd worked it out. Cold air was the classic sign of a haunting. As we stayed there for a few more moments with Luce and Red, I just knew we were going to see Sally again one last time.

"You okay?" Ryan said, frowning at me.

I looked across at the hazy sky over the woods and nodded.

"Come on," I said, seeing that the other four riders had disappeared down the slope and out of our view. "Let's have a great last ride."

I had no idea then, despite my sense of foreboding, quite how crazy the next half an hour was to become.

Rachel, Fern, Liv and Ed were already way ahead of us across the fields. Luce and Red were eager to catch up and fly together across the wonderful space. We descended the slope carefully and then Luce took me into a fabulous flat-out gallop. Red's hooves pounded the soft earth in opposite rhythm to the drumming of our gallop. This was what we lived for. We had gained on the others but they were far, far ahead of us, in the direction of the power station. We followed the line toward it and its cluster of huge cooling towers and jumble of electrical pylons and coils.

Fern and Ed clearly knew where they were going, but there was a rough swathe of a trail that clearly guided us past the various little hillocks and patches of scrub, with long grasses burned beige by the sun.

It was Luce who began tossing his head and made it clear that he didn't want to keep going. We had stopped and started and taken it a little easier, but ten minutes after we had started across the fields I pulled him up. I knew something wasn't right. Ryan had gone ahead, eager to catch up with the others. Luce stood still. He didn't want to go on and he wanted me to know it. I looked ahead at the power station and knew I wanted to get a little closer to it, and maybe even look over the cliffs at the sea.

Luce stamped the ground twice and continued shaking his head. Reluctantly, I dismounted and checked his feet for any stones or sign of lameness. I knew there was nothing physically wrong with him anyway, so I went around to his head and faced him, rubbing his nose and talking to him.

"You're wrecking a great ride," I told him.

I looked into his eyes, and as I did I saw the background of the sky to the east and drew in a sharp breath. Framing my horse's head was a deep, purple-black horizon – so threatening it seemed to be almost bubbling with menace.

There we were, riding along looking at the last lovely clear blue sky of the day we had just enjoyed – and all the time *this* was coming in behind us, like someone drawing a curtain in our wake. None of us had looked the other way. None of us had looked in the direction the weather always came in from, and now the storm had crept up on top of us. And it looked like I was the only one who realized it.

As if to punctuate my realization the first thunder exploded across the fields. It was such an amazing crack that I ducked my head down and clung to the reins, desperate for Luce not to take flight and compound our problems. He wheeled around and reared, but he wasn't leaving me.

I looked ahead for Ryan and was relieved to see he was on his way back to me, eyeing the horizon anxiously.

"We need to get back fast," he shouted. "Fern and Rach have gone to get the others. They're miles in front. I'm guessing we've got ten minutes before that's right above us."

I tried to calm Luce as we saw the first lightning flash. Ryan muttered, "I've never seen lightning like that."

In my head I was counting "five, six, seven, eight, nine.." and then the crack of thunder came and Luce reared. Then Rachel was back with us.

"Fern's with them," she told us. "She said she knows where they can go to be out of it. There's an old barn. What are we going to do?" she wailed.

"Not panic," Ryan said firmly. "We'll make it back."

I sprang into the saddle and Luce and I whirled around as the first fat drop of rain hit my forehead.

"Come on!"

No one needed another invitation and we began the gallop back to the slope, toward the storm. Luce was leading the way, his head tucked down as far as he could manage against the driving wind and rain.

We wasted no time in gaining the slope. Ryan reached the top ahead of us and as Rachel and I reached the flat clearing we were confronted by the sight of Red rearing, right in front of us. Ryan stayed on and whirled around to face Rachel and me, as we struggled to halt our horses beside him. The expression on Ryan's face almost made me let go of the reins, such was the terror in his eyes. I looked to where we were heading – across the clearing to the slope that led back down to the farm – and then I saw it. There, clear to see, was the shadowy outline of a rider, heading right toward us across the open space to the fields, at a full gallop through the storm.

Before I could try and take a closer look I felt the most incredible sensation. For a couple of seconds, it was like my body had turned to ice. My bones, my stomach, my heart. I wondered if I had died right there, at that moment. But as Luce whirled around to face the fields I saw once again, right ahead of me, the ghostly outline of the rider. Our ghost was there, in front of me, a white shadow of herself, riding like the wind in the direction of the slope. Sally's unmistakable braid bounced around her shoulders and a satchel-type bag bounced against her side as she rode on.

But then she stopped. She stopped and she turned to us. We all faced her as the horses pranced and whirled madly in the clearing.

I was amazed to see that the black clouds were now right overhead. I'd never seen weather move so fast. The storm had arrived and it was right above us! I wheeled around in time to see another flash of lightning tear through the sky – a spectacular fork piercing the rumbling purple cloud and striking down into the earth, right at the top of the slope down to the farm.

A scream tore through the sound of the rain. I looked at Rachel. Her mouth was wide open.

"That's where we would have been!" she shrieked. "We would have been right there!"

I turned to face Sally. She was no longer heading for the fields and what would have been safety. I watched as she rode across the clearing and into the woods. We stared as her destiny played out before us and the skies raged above our heads.

I knew when the next lightning strike would come. And I knew where it would come. The three of us were transfixed by the scene unfolding before us, trying to keep the horses together as they pulled and whirled.

"Can we stop her?" Rachel screamed, as Sally and her horse slipped into the trees.

I shook my head.

"It's already happened!"

Ryan was trying to tell us something. He leaned toward us for another try, battling to control Red.

"I think we're supposed to watch," he shouted.

Our last sight of Sally came as she and her horse picked their way in past the first line of trees. The next ten seconds seemed like hours as we waited for it to happen. I didn't want to look, but I couldn't tear my gaze away.

The final devastating bolt of lightning and simultaneous cracking thunder were like nothing I'd ever seen before or would ever see again. The main shaft of lightning was so wide it was like a crack in our world, revealing a view of a new white wilderness beyond it. It hit the earth in the center of the woods and shook the ground under our feet. We saw the orange shaft of flame dart up from the woods as the electricity conducted to the ground, devastating the huge tree. The thunder shocked our bodies as the sound of the splitting tree reached our ears and the rain began to hammer down on us even harder. Then I heard the scream of the terrified horse again. This time, it made perfect sense.

"We have to go and help her!" Rachel cried, her face crumpled and anguished. I looked back at her.

"We can't," I said. I paused a moment. "She's already gone."

I turned to Ryan. He was staring at the woods as the rain flattened his dark curls to his forehead. He urged Red forward, and we began to move tentatively in the direction of the fields as the next lightning strike came far over to the right, way beyond the woods. And beyond us. We were safe, and it looked as if the others, far away on the fields, would be too.

The rain was so heavy that someone dashing to a car a yard way would have been soaked by the time they reached it. The worst of the storm shower was over minutes later. We waited at the top on the ridge, turning the horses back toward the fields so that they weren't facing the heavy rain. The wind had dropped and we didn't need to shout any more. Ryan's phone rang. It was Mr. Vazquez.

"We're all fine," Ryan told his father. "Rachel and Salma … we're just going to get the others now. Back soon."

Rachel got her phone out. "Six missed calls from Dad." She shook her head. "That poor girl."

Sally had shown us her fate. We couldn't have stopped her or changed what had happened. The three of us waited in a line, our gazes often drawn over to the trees, their deathly secret finally revealed to us. Rachel was next to me in the silent lineup. She shook her head slowly.

"I can't believe that," she said eventually. "Why did she go into the woods in a storm?" she paused. "Why? They were heading for the fields. She would have been okay that way."

"It would have been quick," Ryan said. "They wouldn't have known anything about it. They fell into that pit and the lightning would have just taken them away."

I closed my eyes and thought about it. A flash and they had both gone. I truly hoped that was how it had been. But everyone had thought she had run away, for all these years. Or did Tom know deep down that Sally had never made it out? I thought about what Rachel said. Sally had been heading for the fields. We had seen her gallop to the top of the slope. But she had stopped, long enough to stop us heading into the lightning strike. She had saved us, but not herself. Suddenly I saw it all clearly. She had changed the present but was unable to evade her own destiny. She had turned and headed for those trees. She could have gotten away, but she headed for those trees. Every bone in Sally's body must have been willing her to gallop down the slope, but she had chosen the woods, to hide – and to wait for Tom. I was certain of that. I took a deep breath.

"She saved us," I murmured.

Liv, Ed and Fern were soon heading toward us across the fields. They were riding side by side along the grass trail. I smiled, relieved at the sight of my friends and unable to really think about or comprehend what had happened just before. I could see Liv's face now, her usually bouncy curls plastered to her face. They all waved to us, and we watched them reach the bottom of the slope.

"Thank goodness you're okay!" Liv shouted. "We thought you'd had it with that lightning bolt up there. Did you see it?"

Chapter 10

Ryan and I had put all the pieces of the jigsaw together, with all the help we could have wished for from our tragic friend from the past. As it grew dark on our last night, everyone was safe, in our time anyway, and Mr. Vazquez had just about recovered his composure after losing us all in the storm.

"I just wish Tom could have seen her again," I said to Ryan.

"I know," he replied. "But at least we worked out why she was in the woods. We saw her change her mind. She couldn't just go without him ... should we tell him that, though?" Ryan thought for a moment. "Maybe he's already worked it out," he said.

"But that means she died because she tried to wait for him." I shook my head. "I'm just so glad we've found her now – and that lovely horse."

Morgan and Peterson had solved that part of the mystery – the saddest possible outcome for Sally and Tom.

We were down in the sitting room, waiting for the others to join us. They were taking forever making a hot drink for everyone in the kitchen. Mr. Vazquez had gotten so fed up waiting for his he'd gone to try and find out what was going on. I heard Liv say, "Sorry!" and then Mr. Vazquez call, "Good-night people," and then go up the stairs.

It was half an hour after the police had left. The bones were the remains of a sturdy male horse – about 15 plus hands high, and a young female. They were certain of that now.

With her father afraid of the woods and sworn to never set foot in them, Sally had taken a chance, and paid for it with her life.

Ryan and I had given our full statements about the discovery of the bones and, amazingly, Morgan had told us that on that night in 1962 there had been a massive storm. He had found it documented in the local history of the nearby town. It had brought down power lines and caused flash flooding. The un-forecasted storm had struck on a Friday night in August. I'd lost track of the days we had been away, but tonight, the night of our storm, was a Friday night in August too.

We heard a soft knock at the door. Ryan got up to answer it and I followed. Tom was standing on the doorstep.

"Come in," Ryan said and Tom stepped into the hall. He was smiling.

Ryan led Tom into the living room as the others burst out of the kitchen. Ryan placed a finger to his mouth. Rachel nodded and they followed us into the sitting room quietly.

Tom sat down and we all settled around him. He seemed pleased to see Fern and Edward.

"Glad you all got to know each other," he said. Then he turned to Ryan and me. "Thanks for bringing Sally back to me. Thanks for finding her," he said.

"We're sorry she didn't get away," Ryan said. He wasn't going to tell Tom that Sally nearly did get away, that she changed her mind.

"I don't think she was supposed to get away," Tom said. "Maybe she was thinking of hiding out in those woods, hoping I'd find her there. Maybe she would have gotten away if it wasn't for me ... but there's no use thinking about that too much."

I was so glad Tom had come to that conclusion. He had obviously thought of every possible scenario since they had found Sally.

"Maybe he would have found her and brought her back to the farm, locked her up for good – and her life would have been far worse."

I nodded. Then I had a thought. "I'm just going to get something," I said.

I slipped upstairs to Ryan's room and felt under the

bed for the bundle we had found in the loft. Retrieving it, I gently pulled out the happy photo of Sally from under the string. I went back downstairs and handed it to Tom, looking at Ryan as I did so. His bright and encouraging expression told me I was doing the right thing.

"We found it in the attic."

Tom looked at the photo in amazement. Then he stared at it for a long time before clutching it to his chest and staring up at the ceiling.

"What will you do?" I asked him. "Will you have to leave the house now?"

Tom nodded.

"The police said I have to, but I'm ready now," he told us. "I'll let them look after me. I don't need to be here any more." Tom smiled.

"I think you're right," I told him.

Tom left a while later. He hugged and thanked us, still clutching the photograph to his heart.

"He was called Nelson … Sally's horse," Tom told us, as he turned to go.

Ryan and I smiled, and I felt sad once again.

We all stayed up late, wanting to spend as much time with our new friends as we could, talking the whole thing over and over. Liv was close to Ed on one of the sofas.

It was sad saying goodbye to Ed and Fern. Liv found a

way to say goodbye to Ed over in the yard, alone. When they came back around to the front of the house they were both smiling. No doubt I would find out later what happened. In detail!

Ryan and I went out to the yard to say good-night. Luce was his usual self, eyeballing me in his unique way, mischief just there, lurking in the background.

"I wish we just had one more day here," I said to Ryan, "one more day to ride and chill out. To go up that slope and not wonder what's going to happen when we get to the top of it."

"Yeah," Ryan agreed. "A ghost-free day."

I laughed. "There is one thing I want to do tomorrow," I added. "Will you come up to the woods tomorrow morning with me? I want to take some flowers, for Sally – and for Nelson."

Ryan nodded and we were both quiet for a while.

"I don't know about you," Ryan said eventually, smiling at me. "But after this, I'd really like to go on a shoot and not uncover any nightmares from the past."

I grinned. "There's not much chance of that if my boy is with us." I rubbed the front of Luce's face and he pushed at me playfully.

"Then we'll have to leave him behind," Ryan said. I looked at him in time to see my "boyfriend" trying to hide a grin from me.

"No. Way!" I said, grinning.

I looked at him and he looked back at me, smiling and looking, for just a moment too long.

"What?" I asked

He looked down for a moment.

"Nothing," he said, smiling at me some more.